DATE DUE

DEC 5 1986			

DEMCO 38-297

THE IMMIGRANT HERITAGE OF AMERICA
SERIES

Cecyle S. Neidle, Editor

The Radical Immigrant

By SALLY M. MILLER
University of the Pacific

Twayne Publishers, Inc. :: New York

Library of Congress Cataloging in Publication Data

Miller, Sally M   1937–
    The radical immigrant.

    (The Immigrant heritage of America series)
    Bibliography: p.
    1. Radicalism—United States—History.
2. United States—Emigration and immigration—History.
I. Title.
HN90.R3M5   322.4'4   73-15847
ISBN 0-8057-3266-7

To the Memory of F.J.M.
and All for which He Stood

Contents

Preface

Acknowledgments

Preface

THIS IS A STUDY OF A NUMBER OF IMMIGRANTS TO THE UNITED States who offered fundamental criticisms of their adopted nation. Covering the century of immigration from 1820 to 1920, this study focuses upon various radicals among the immigrants. While analyzing their ideas and careers, the book places its emphasis not upon the organizations they built but upon the individuals themselves. The goal is to illustrate the continuity and change in their radical critiques over the decades. Divergent figures are explored in order to demonstrate the richness of the traditions they represented. A broad definition of the word "radical" is utilized. This allows for the consideration of individuals as varied as Alexander Berkman, who was finally exiled because of his ideas, and Carl Schurz, who eventually fit comfortably into the mainstream of American politics.

Men and women were chosen for inclusion essentially on the basis of their prominence and influence in regard to radical points of view. Some promising candidates were rejected because of minimal source material. Others were excluded because they were overshadowed by more influential colleagues or because their roles were deemed to be only incidental in a life played out elsewhere. While great effort has been made to insure meaningful selections, it is possible that faulty judgment has resulted in debatable inclusions or exclusions. If so, the author must bear the responsibility.

A selection process of this nature eventually confronts the issue of typicality. The question as to whether these individuals were representative of the radical immigrants of their era can not be definitively resolved. Citing an average radical, on the contemporary as well as the historical stage, is fraught with difficulties, as psychiatrist Kenneth Kenniston remarks. Variety and idiosyncracy abound. Therefore the beclouded issue of typicality must inevitably be sidestepped.

What should emerge, however, is the wealth of ideas, ideals, and insights that compose the American background, due in some degree to the presence in our history of these individuals. So often despised or, perhaps worse in their own eyes, ignored, they left our country the richer for their struggles.

SALLY M. MILLER

November, 1972

Acknowledgments

AN ABILITY TO CONCEPTUALIZE AND TO ANALYZE IS BARELY A
sufficient foundation for undertaking research in history. Of
enormous importance are the following: a willingness to read
and review the same material unnumbered times from different
angles; an absence of allergies to archival dust; an indifference
to print stain on the fingers; an interest in sifting through
materials somewhat related to the topic but often producing
little; and an enthusiasm for travel. All of this implies an
ability to hang on and endure. Most vital of all is a belief
that, for some reason, the project is worth it all.

That historical scholarship is possible is due to the existence
of repositories of all types of data. My thanks are offered to
the staffs of the following libraries who, either via correspondence
or through on-the-spot assistance, proved to be professional
helpmates: the Library of Congress, the New York Public
Library, the New-York Historical Society, the University of
Michigan, the Chicago Historical Society, the University of
Chicago, the Historical Society of Pennsylvania, the State Historical Society of Wisconsin, the Ohio Historical Society, the
Indiana State Library, the Indiana Historical Society, Vassar
College, the Massachusetts Historical Society, the Milwaukee
County Historical Society, Tamiment Institute of New York City,
and the Public Library of Cincinnati and Hamilton County.

In the early stages of the research, including especially the
hunting down of the location of vital material, two former
students, Hugh A. Linstrom and James H. Buckley, were help-
ful assistants. Others who assisted in translating some of the
German materials were Mary T. McAdams and George Wegerle.
The manuscript was typed by two former students, Sherry A.

Holm and Kathryn J. Tobias. I offer my warm appreciation to all of them and the hope that the effort was in some way worthwhile for each.

The editor of the series, Dr. Cecyle S. Neidle, has been exceedingly generous with her time and patient beyond what an author might expect. She has shown great dedication to making the final draft superior to the original. I extend my deep gratitude to her.

I am happy to offer special thanks to colleagues who were kind enough to read the manuscript, in various stages, in whole or in part, and to provide me with their professional criticisms. My warm thanks to Professor Robert S. Fogarty of Antioch College, Professor James M. Bergquist of Villanova University, Professor William G. Whittaker of Gonzaga University, Professor Stuart B. Kaufman of the University of Maryland, Professor Donald H. Grubbs of the University of the Pacific, and especially to Professor Joseph Levitt of the University of Ottawa, Canada, whose advice and comments have been in the background of all of my publications. My most profound sense of debt is to Margaret J. Keranen of Stockton, California, who, with a keen editorial eye and an apparent inability to be bored, saw the manuscript through to completion. The responsibility for errors and weaknesses is, of course, my own.

The reference librarians of the University of the Pacific were indispensable assistants throughout the course of the research. I am grateful to Judith A. Gipson, J. Frank Jones, and especially Laura M. Boyer. Her boundless enthusiasm allowed for the tracking down of seemingly hopelessly lost documentation. Finally, the University of the Pacific kindly granted me Faculty Research Awards in 1970 and in 1971 which were expended on travel expenses to various archives across the country, the acquisition of primary source material, and some of the costs involved in manuscript preparation. Such vital assistance, signifying the university's recognition of the inherent connection between teaching and research, is deeply appreciated.

CHAPTER I

The Immigrant and Radicalism

AMERICAN HISTORY IS A STORY OF IMMIGRATION, AND THAT IS especially so during the nineteenth century. That century witnessed the greatest mass migration of all times. From the end of the Napoleonic Wars to the Treaty of Versailles, intra-European and transoceanic migration resulted in the uprooting of millions of people. Over fifty million Europeans emigrated and settled in developing countries such as Australia, Canada, Argentina, Brazil, and the United States. Three-fifths of these migrants came to the United States. While statistics fail to indicate the proportion of those who re-emigrated or who migrated seasonally, clearly this enormous mass served to populate the American nation, work its land and industry, enrich its intellectual and cultural life, and modify the American experience.[1]

The transportation revolution of the nineteenth century made distant areas of the world accessible while, at the same time, the abolition of traditional political and economic restraints resulted in mobility for the masses of Europe. In each generation, stimulated primarily by economic factors, an emigrant stream poured out of Europe. In the third decade of the nineteenth century, the British Isles and Scandinavia began to witness the departure of their working classes. Toward mid-century, Central Europe also experienced such an exodus and, from the eighties to the First World War, emigration from Eastern and Southern Europe became commonplace.

A series of technical inventions in England in the late eighteenth century enormously increased that nation's industrial potential. By the early nineteenth century the growing industrial might had revolutionized work habits and living conditions for the English masses. Those formerly employed in shops and cottage industries worked within the harsh discipline of the factory system. Their lives, whether in new mill towns or in expanding cities, became increasingly squalid. With the repeal of the restrictions on emigration in 1825, English workers began to leave the motherland for the New World. Joined in the thirties and forties by the hungry Irish, the British eventually made up the largest block of immigrants to the United States of any nationality.[2]

In Central Europe, the German-speaking states drew together for purposes of free trade during the twenties and thirties. Industrial development supplanted the traditional handicraft system and transformed the skilled artisan into a factory hand. In agriculture, the abolition of most forms of feudal obligations turned Prussian peasants into a landless agrarian proletariat and led other German peasants into overmortgaged commercial farming. A series of depressions, culminating in the forties in the last major European famine, resulted in severe economic crisis. Emigration, apparently the only viable choice of hundreds of thousands of German working people, followed.[3]

Eastern and southern Europeans emigrated in the last two decades of the nineteenth century and in the early years of the twentieth century. Italians from the southern provinces of the newly unified kingdom of Italy, Slavs of various nationalities from the heterogeneous Austro-Hungarian Empire and the Balkans, and Jews, Poles, and other minorities from the Russian Empire were the dominant groups. While conditions varied, the most basic factor leading to emigration "... was everywhere the same, namely, one of dislocation resulting from the breakup of the age-old peasant economy."[4] As in Central Europe, the end of feudalism had resulted in the subdivision of peasant property into inadequate holdings.

Simultaneously, the inroads of industry eliminated the need for craftsmen as ready-made goods and mechanization appeared in northern Italy, Bohemia, and western Russia. Among the minorities in the Russian Empire, restrictive legislation, long-term conscription, and pogroms impelled escape. By the end of the century, these factors led to the emigration of millions and to the domination of American immigration statistics by eastern and southern Europeans.[5]

The American government first began to compile statistics on immigration in the 1820's. At that time and in the subsequent decades, immigration rolls were composed nearly exclusively of English, Irish, Germans, and somewhat later, of Scandinavians. Even in 1886, seventy-six percent of the arrivals were identified by immigration authorities as northwestern European in nationality. In that year newcomers from eastern and southern Europe formed twenty-two percent of the incoming wave. In 1900 they numbered more than two-thirds of the arrivals.[6]

The origin of the immigrants was a significant factor in their reception by the American public and in their own adaptation problems in the new environment. Americans took for granted the dominance of their English-derived institutions and mores, and immigrant cultures at variance with the core pattern faced a less than cordial populace. Differences in language, religion, appearance, or habits were perceived by Americans as threatening or as inferior. When such variations became endemic, hostility and prejudice became commonplace.

The ease of adaptability for the immigrant groups depended upon their particular backgrounds and also upon the time of their arrival in the United States. Emigrants from Western Europe, especially from England, experienced the least difficulty in the acculturation process. For the English-speaking, no language barrier existed. Moreover, the demands and conditions of early industrialism encountered here by the English were already familiar to them. Indeed, in many instances, English workers assumed the lead in imparting skills to Americans and in showing them how to cope with the changing environment. Any nineteenth-century immigrant who came from an urban-industrial milieu, even if he faced a language barrier, was confronted with relatively few adaptation crises in the American urban scene.

However, those immigrants whose formative experiences had occurred within an agrarian or rural framework were unprepared for the urban confrontation. As the decades wore on, the majority of the immigrants, except for many of the Italians and most of the Jews, represented an agrarian *Völkerwanderung* whose migration almost invariably ended in an urban setting. These people possessed values shaped by their agrarian and handicraft backgrounds and by their generally authoritarian religious frameworks. They brought with them psychological perspectives honed in peasant societies and, therefore, inappropriate to the urban centers where so many settled. Additionally, away from the Old Country, the traditional interdependence and primary relationships were not always easy to reproduce. Not surprisingly, the result could be social dislocation.

The degree of maturity of the American economy was another crucial factor affecting immigrant adaptation. All newcomers participated in the evolution of the decentralized, rural nation into a consolidated, industrial country. Indeed, the process could not have occurred at such a rapid rate had it not been for the growing labor force. The early arrivals, those with skills and training, often were able to choose their work, while even those whose specific technical expertise was not in demand could find some diversity of opportunity.[7] In the later decades, however, the scope narrowed. Those emigrating after the Civil War, during the rapidly accelerating pace of industrialization, possessing no skills useful to the economy, found that only their muscle was marketable. With their Old World skills rejected, they entered only those pursuits which required neither knowledge nor capital. They provided the bulk of the manpower and supplied the changing needs of the American economy.

The background, aspirations, and experiences of the immigrants, particularly as the decades passed, might easily have been expected to breed docility in the newcomers. Nevertheless, by the turn of the twentieth century the view of the immigrant held by the native-born and the older immigrants was that the immigrant often challenged American institutions. He came to be seen as a danger to indigenous traditions. His image became that of a political agitator, despite the basic economic conservatism of most immigrants. The immigrants came to represent upheaval and riot. Very frequently, the stereotype of the immigrant was the radical.

In the last twenty-five years of the nineteenth century, a combination of events growing out of evolving American social conditions, led to the strengthening of that stereotype. As an integral part of labor's struggle to win a secure base in collective bargaining, industrial warfare flourished. Many of the bloody upheavals of those years involved immigrant participants. As a result, the immigrant was blamed for encouraging worker discontent, increasing social tensions, and fomenting class hatreds.

Incidents that were woven into the tapestry of nativism began with the Molly Maguires. The terrorism they produced in the Pennsylvania coal mining areas in the 1870's, was one instance which contributed to the impression that foreigners were apt to be dangerous radicals. The railroad strikes across half the continent in 1877, threatening the entire transportation network of the nation, increased apprehension and the need for a scapegoat. Fears of foreigners heightened. In 1886 the Chicago Haymarket Affair in the midst of the eight-hour movement (which was only incidentally supported by local German anarchists) was interpreted to be convincing circumstantial evidence of alien disruption. New immigrants represented a threat to the American system. Revolution with a foreign accent might be imminent unless aliens with their radical notions and mysterious plans were denied entry to the United States.[8]

In 1901 the assassination of President William McKinley by a native American of eastern European extraction seared the stereotype into the public's consciousness. The immediate effect of the assassination on federal immigration policies was the first restrictionist legislation based on political beliefs: an adherent of anarchism or regicide was barred from entry to the United States.

Thereafter, the American public seemed more confident and less anxious over possible foreign tampering with established traditions, but the excitement and hysteria of the First World War revived the worst fears of the Haymarket days. The immigrant once again became the scapegoat for a national loss of optimism and recurrent social tensions. The Red Scare with its mass arrests and deportations of aliens followed. Soon comprehensive restrictionist legislation excluded foreign radicals and revolutionaries and, indeed, almost all immigrants. The door was closed to the Promised Land, reversing a traditional American policy, essentially because of the strong identification of immigrant and radical in public opinion.[9]

Refutation of this erroneous identification became the task of the writers of immigration histories during the first quarter of the twentieth century. Few professional historians had focused upon immigration prior to the 1920's, leaving the field to amateur historians whose major goal was often the glorification of their own ethnic groups. Filiopietism, the veneration of group accomplishments, was supported by the mushrooming ethnic historical societies. Filiopietistic writers extolled the contributions of their group to the nation. They insisted upon their unique "racial" gifts to the development of the United States, while simultaneously each one emphasized the moderation and patience of his own people. All connections between the individual group and obtrusive political behavior were minimized by the filiopietists. In their denials and omissions, they produced a selective history which, while at least providing focus on these neglected groups, viewed immigrants through a distorted prism.[10]

The first professional historians who dealt directly and analytically with immigrant history began their work in the twenties. The major pioneers, second or third generation Americans, were George M. Stephenson, Theodore C. Blegen,

Marcus Lee Hansen, and Carl F. Wittke. These historians, in laying the foundation for the new field, disregarded the unscientific racial interpretations and the excessive pietistic glorifications of the past. They examined the immigrant experience and heritage, usually focusing upon their own forebears, the Swedish, the Norwegian, and the German. They saw the achievement of their people to be the expansion and building of the United States. By World War II, sufficient groundwork had been provided by these historians for more specialized studies to appear. But despite the effort to dislodge the traditional impression of the immigrant as a problem to the United States, the distorted image of the immigrant as radical had not been undermined.[11]

The frontal assault on the stereotype occurred with the publication in 1951 of *The Uprooted,* Oscar Handlin's Pulitzer Prize winning study of the immigration process. Handlin argued that most immigrants were conservative in their political and social outlooks and actions due to their formative experiences and the subsequent dislocation of the migration process. With so many of them originating in comparatively backward societies, their dependence on tradition and authority was fixed. The immigration pattern, essentially disruptive, intensified those needs, and thus, the immigrant tended to remain aloof from the various radical movements of his era. In his highly impressionistic analysis, Handlin traced the immigrants' experiences and even their emotions, and demonstrated the way in which a sense of group consciousness emerged from the need to survive.[12]

Handlin succeeded in adding balance to our understanding of the immigrant. He undermined the stereotype of the radical immigrant. However, in his effort to destroy that image, Handlin created a contrasting stereotype which resulted once more in a warped view of the so-called typical immigrant. First of all, Handlin's picture certainly did not fit all immigrant groups as he concentrated on immigrants from Eastern Europe. Secondly, some of the strengths immigrants developed as a result of their adversities, such as group consciousness, in fact sometimes became direct routes to non-conservative actions.

Among the various immigrant groups, the social dislocation of the English and some of the Germans was minimal due to their Old World experiences in an urban-industrial milieu.

Urbanized Jews and Italians also met with less dislocation than has been implied. In many instances, these two groups did not sacrifice their primary group memberships upon their migration. In Boston, New York, Chicago, and other cities where many Italians and Jews settled, familiar situations were frequently recreated and group relationships transplanted. Thus traditional family, neighbor, and other primary relationships continued in a new setting, decreasing the degree of alienation and insecurity.

Even among immigrants who arrived directly from rural environments, social dislocation could be minimized. Group consciousness could be maintained by Bohemians, Poles, and others who might live together in mill towns or in little Pragues or Warsaws of large American cities. Their interrelation with one another gave them a foundation of strength from which they were able to confront new challenges and act together forcefully as occasion demanded. Thus, as recent scholarship has demonstrated, even the most village-oriented Europeans transplanted to the bustling industrial environment of the New World were capable of militant actions. They could respond to those individual radical immigrants whose arrival in each generation has never been denied.[13]

The radical immigrant leader was a man or woman who was committed to the profound restructuring of society. He or she perceived inequities and injustices in the status quo, and demanded social transformation. Within this broad definition are encompassed radicals of various hues, whose paths frequently meandered and whose directions sometimes became modified. Often these radicals had become alienated from Western society prior to their emigration from the Old World, although some of them became radicalized solely as a result of American experiences. Their critical judgments led them to propagandize, organize, and act to implement necessary changes. Some chose to work within the existing political and social structure in order to bring about the desired transformation through legal and gradual means while a number eventually settled for mild reforms rather than wholesale change. Others sought disengagement from the American framework by building communities of their own design separate from society such as the one at New Harmony.

From the 1820's to the 1920's, a steady trickle of radicals came to the United States as part of the larger flood of immigrants. In the antebellum period, a time when the United States had both open space and wide employment opportunities, instances were not uncommon of immigrants settling in relatively isolated groups. For some, the goal was the construction of separatist colonies whose experiences might be an example of the good life that the larger society could emulate. In the old Northwest especially, the communitarian impulse was displayed in almost every state until the eve of the Civil War. In this same period, radical immigrants offered leadership to the workers of the growing cities of the eastern seaboard. The would-be leaders usually looked back to the English industrial experience in order to organize the American labor force to deal with emerging conditions. Simultaneously, a handful of women among these radical immigrants attempted to challenge native American assumptions about women's role in society. They prodded the incipient feminist movement to expand its attacks on the status quo.

In the decade prior to the Civil War, a small group of German Forty-eighter revolutionaries arrived in the New World with definite convictions about the inadequacies of the American Republic. Armed with detailed programs for political, economic, and social change, they sought to introduce their ideas into their ethnic group. A number of them, particularly the less doctrinaire, met with some success in integrating the German community into American society by alignment with progressive forces of the eighteen-fifties.

In the period between the Civil War and the First World War, when the United States required a large, unskilled working class, untutored immigrant labor introduced new tactics to the organized labor movement. While often neglected by the unions, the immigrant workers nevertheless were responsible for widening labor's horizons as to means and goals.

These same decades witnessed the mushrooming of various organized movements which, however minuscule, denounced the most fundamental political and social precepts of American society. Led by immigrant intellectuals of socialist or anarchist persuasions, these radical movements sought to revolutionize the United States. Theirs were the most far-ranging immigrant-based challenges to hallowed American beliefs. The subsequent closing of the era of immigration was not unrelated to these radicals.

The presence of the radical immigrant, his numbers often exaggerated and his designs frequently distorted beyond frankly acknowledged purposes, became a cause of American rejection of immigration. The history of this maligned and neglected first-generation American follows.

CHAPTER II

Antebellum Radical Immigrants

NINETEENTH-CENTURY WESTERN MAN FACED DRASTICALLY CHANG-
ing economic, social, and political conditions. The breakdown
of traditional structures, occurring first in the British Isles, then
in Belgium, France, the United States, and other countries,
affected eventually even those who lived in relative isolation.
Industrialization, with the accompanying rapid urbanization,
altered the means of earning a living for masses of people.
Craftsmen and artisans in domestic industries became replace-
able wage earners in large-scale enterprises. Joined at work by
wives and children, they were subject to economic forces beyond
their control while, at the same time, family life disintegrated.[1]

After the Napoleonic Wars, degradation of the English working people reached its nadir. Insecure employment, deplorable
living conditions, and the possibility of escape overseas led to
mass migration starting in the third decade of the century.
Simultaneously, a number of critics emerged who were angry
and impatient over these by-products of social change. While
impoverishment had been routine in preindustrial society, the
new conditions of squalor could hardly be termed customary
or inevitable.

The assumptions which motivated these men and women
stemmed from the Enlightenment of the eighteenth century.
They believed in a rational world in which mankind, if freed
of restraints, could achieve unceasing progress. They were
hostile to governmental, religious, and other forces which obstructed individual human potential. Convinced that inhumane
social conditions need not be tolerated, some of the critics

[23]

sought to reshape radically the structure of English society, while others chose to build the good society elsewhere.

Early in the nineteenth century, most Old World critics viewed the New World as an inviting area. The United States offered conditions that seemed to permit empirical experimentation. The young nation had more open space than it needed; unlimited acreage awaited those who would come. In addition, the United States promised relative political freedom. Also it lacked a state church. Both of these factors were taken to indicate flexibilty. Such intellectual openness and fluid attitudes were peculiarly attractive to those who wished to build from scratch; American citizens were not mentally bound by centuries-old habits of mind; nor were they beyond persuasion to new ideas and paths. Hence the American mind, as well as the land itself, was a magnet drawing potential reformers.

As a final attraction, the American social structure offered a fluidity unknown to post-Napoleonic Europe. The youthfulness of American society precluded tight class lines, and although class barriers were mushrooming, recognizable divisions lay in the future. Thus, from various angles, conditions in the United States beckoned to experimenters, reformers, and radicals of different persuasions. Such an irresistible opportunity was not easy to reject.[2]

In the third decade of the nineteenth century the United States was not yet an industrial nation but it was already beginning to approach the "take-off" into self-sustaining growth. By 1820 both the mechanization of industry and the creation of the factory system had been initiated. The War of 1812 had stimulated American businessmen to exploit existing resources and had transformed the American importer into a manufacturer. Thereafter, the development of internal improvements—turnpikes and canals as well as the use of steam-driven riverboats—enabled manufactured products and produce to be hauled quickly and easily between population centers. This revolution in transportation united the various regions of the country commercially and paved the way for the merchant capitalist. The latter, who usually lacked technical expertise, felt compelled to cut costs drastically in order to compete with goods that had once again begun to flow from Europe.

Costs could most easily be lowered through decreased wage scales, and consequently, in the 1820's, the American worker saw his standard of living threatened. In addition to reduced wages, working conditions in general worsened sufficiently to stir the craftsmen to action. This period has been described by John R. Commons and his pioneering associates in labor history as demonstrating "signs of awakening." The factory system began to usurp household and shop manufacturing, making the craftsmen's skills superfluous. The employer turned into a distant figure to the workmen, while anonymity and alienation became commonplace in the lives of American workers. As a feeling of helplessness deepened, the worker and the nation, too, began to show the "many signs of congestion and pauperism" that marked the English scene under early industrialism.[3]

Though the full transformation of the American system from an agrarian-based handicraft economy was far from complete in the antebellum years, to some observers from England, even in the 1820's the foundations for industrial capitalism were already visible. Shortly after his emigration from England, Robert Dale Owen, the eldest son of Robert Owen, remarked on the similarity of workingmen's complaints in the two countries and expressed the fear that the United States had already embarked on England's path of "wealth and misery."[4]

Individuals such as the Owenses were well prepared to recognize both the promise and the pathos of the developing economy: the future prosperity of the nation and the existing exploitation of the working masses. Because the Owenses had experienced in their native environment the problems now emerging in the United States, they could see the dimensions of the unfolding crisis. Therefore, it was not surprising that from such immigrants solutions and reforms emanated, sometimes in terms of very radical social change. But the possibility existed that they might magnify or distort conditions, or that they might find themselves in an unreal realm, unable to attract supporters or to confront substantive issues.[5]

However appropriate their insights into American conditions may have been, these early reformers of the nineteenth century were determined to prevent or, in many cases, to check the sufferings and inequities of developing industrialism they had observed elsewhere.

Communitarianism

When Robert Dale Owen (1801-1877) disembarked in New York City on November 7, 1825, his twenty-fourth birthday, his mood was buoyant and eager. How auspicious to launch his life in the New World on such a day! The scenery was even more impressive than he had imagined and he felt that he "... had reached the Canaan of my hopes." Owen, no ordinary immigrant lad, was preceded by his father's fame. Armed with letters of introduction, and flanked by his father and his disciples, young Owen was entranced by the cordial reception that was given them in New York and Philadelphia. A week after his arrival before a Philadelphia court he declared his intention to seek American citizenship.[6]

Robert Dale was impatient to reach southern Indiana and the New Harmony communitarian colony established by his father several months earlier. During his two months' journey from New York to Indiana, by stagecoach and keelboat and finally on horseback, he had whiled away the days of travel and the weeks of delay by discussing with his companions the appropriate practices of the inhabitants and the costumes to be worn in New Harmony, the desirability of a colony newspaper, and the proper pedagogical methods. In quiet moments he poured over Charles Fourier's writings, which he deemed insightful but somewhat impractical. Robert Dale confided to his diary that the hardships and exposure were salutary experiences.

All appear fairly satisfied and I am convinced that they could not have had a better preparation. Now they would be satisfied in

Harmony and become useful members. Otherwise they would have found it inconvenient and would not have been able to do anything for themselves.[7]

Young Owen at once assumed heavy responsibilities in New Harmony. While he was familiar with administrative duties at the elder Owen's New Lanark mills, he was nevertheless an uncertain and insecure young man. As he would later acknowledge, Robert Dale Owen lacked decisiveness at this stage of his life, and the result was both a healthy open-mindedness and an unfortunate naiveté. That there was so much responsibility waiting for him in itself did not augur well for the future of the colony.[8]

The eldest of Robert Owen's four sons had been influenced profoundly by his father. Robert Dale had absorbed his father's general outlook, characterized by optimism, pragmatism, and a paternalistic reformist bent. He shared his father's belief in reason and his religious skepticism. He also accepted many of his father's specific ideas on means for the improvement of the environment, on the need for universal education, and on the inadequacies of capitalism. Above all, he was convinced ". . . that the essential remedy for the suffering which I witnessed around me was, as my father declared it to be, the substitution of cooperative industry for competitive labor." The intensity with which the young man held to this view may be traced to the trauma he experienced upon his first visit to a mill in England as a boy of twelve. After accompanying his father on an inspection tour, he could never forget the sight of children his own age employed ten to fourteen hours per day, breathing polluted mill air and facing corporal punishment from overseers. In fact, he wrote, it ". . . haunted my dreams."[9]

Other influences upon Robert Dale stemmed from his education at Hofwyl, near Berne, Switzerland, where he was subjected to the Pestalozzian methods of Philipp Emanuel von Fellenberg. There Owen was exposed to a broad curriculum, from classics to gymnastics and manual labor. Adjacent to this school for the sons of the European aristocracy and the wealthy, an industrial and agricultural school was conducted by Fellenberg for indigent boys. Class rigidity, within a paternalistic frame of reference, was accompanied by self-government within the college. Young Owen's later educational endeavors lay within the Fellenberg pattern.[10]

Two nineteenth-century philosophies, Fourier's utopianism and Jeremy Bentham's utilitarianism, were reflected in Robert Dale Owen's thought. What particularly attracted Owen to Fourier was his pedagogical program, specifically infant schools. Young Owen, initially sympathetic due to the New Lanark infant education pioneered by his father, agreed with Fourier that children should be housed within the educational institution rather than within the confines of the family in order to avoid dilution of the school's influence. He also believed that a program of education must commence at an early age, three at the latest, and that the educational experience must be relevant to life and embrace all aspects of society.[11] From Jeremy Bentham, a sometime partner of his father's, Robert Dale came to assume that utility was the test of virtue, that enlightened selfishness formed a basis for moral behavior, and that the goals of a desirable social order should be the greatest happiness of the greatest number.[12] Thus, Robert Dale as a young adult viewed the world through a prism reflecting Pestalozzian, Fourierist, Benthamite, and most especially, Owenist ideas.

The senior Robert Owen, one of the most successful "mercantilist aristocrats" to come to the surface in the English industrial revolution, had acquired fame as a reformer. Owen, who at the age of twenty had assumed management of the New Lanark mills and village, had lost interest in profit-making. Apparently lacking real genius for business, but able to seize opportunities in an era rampant with them, the self-made Owen became obsessed by the plight of the mill workers. He shaped New Lanark into a model company town, where he successfully demonstrated that decent conditions, shorter hours, and fair wages could be made profitable. Convinced that improved industrial conditions were only a first step, he erected a school system dedicated to a fundamental reformation of character. Schools based on kindness and stressing the utilitarian would ultimately transform the quality of human life, Owen believed; education from the cradle to the grave was the direct route.[13]

Possibly as early as 1812 Robert Owen had known of the German Rappite religious community at Harmony, Indiana, and in 1820 he wrote Father George Rapp to inquire of ". . . the practical inconveniences which arise from changing society from a state of private to public property under the peculiar circumstances by which your colonies have been surrounded."[14] When the Rappites decided to return to Pennsylvania and offered Harmony for sale in 1824, Owen could not bypass what, according to his son, he felt would be a ". . . vast chance for social reform." The United States, Owen wrote, ought to prove receptive to his new system of small but viable communities living cooperatively on an agrarian-industrial foundation. Individuals living together would thrive by sharing responsibilities and wealth. He envisioned a multiplicity of similar colonies in the relatively unsettled Old Northwest.[15]

The communitarianism of Robert Owen dovetailed with an established American tradition. At the very moment when the religious dimension of American communitarianism was beginning to weaken, Owen's social system imposed itself upon a corner of a western state. His enthusiastic welcome by the press, the public, and even by the President, seemed propitious.[16]

In April, 1825, a so-called preliminary society, a "halfway house," Owen called it, was organized at newly christened New Harmony. Because of his belief that men were shaped by their environment, Owen thought that distinct family structures and individual autonomy must be retained until community consciousness and mutual interests developed. He anticipated that an atmosphere of cooperation would evolve after two years, at which time the new system of full equality could be initiated. In June he departed for England and upon his return the following January, he announced that the one thousand residents who had flocked to New Harmony shared a communal spirit.

The emancipation from ignorance, superstition, individual property, and irrational religion was about to occur.[17]

The emergent community, rough-hewn, burdened with a housing shortage, producing less than it consumed, nonetheless in superficial ways appeared to be thriving. The days were filled with agricultural, mechanical, and craft pursuits, often at an uncertain pace. The evenings were spent in business meetings, social and cultural events. Robert Dale Owen joined the teaching staff consisting of European Pestalozzians such as William Phiquepal d'Arusmont and Joseph Neef. Young Owen modified school practices by prohibiting punishment and introducing drilling, and one pupil, in a memoir sixty years later, remembered most vividly the military aspects of his New Harmony education.[18]

As an editor of the weekly *New Harmony Gazette*, Robert Dale joined a staff which included his brother William. He was anxious to expand the scope of the *Gazette's* concerns. The paper had focused upon the community experiment and its daily events, emphasizing its masthead declaration, "Individuality detracts largely from the sum of human happiness."[19] Robert Dale Owen quickly broadened the paper's horizons. He deepened its skeptical tone through attacks upon organized religion, and he expanded coverage of educational matters, even obtaining contributions from Fellenberg in Switzerland.[20] He introduced material relating to national affairs, such as general discussions of slavery and of the role of the family in industrial society. The newspaper began to overcome its monthly deficits as he widened its readership by sending it unrequested to prominent individuals. Soon subscriptions circulated throughout the United States and even in England and Scotland, and the *Gazette* was the best known paper in the West.[21]

Robert Dale Owen's views of the new social system were most fully developed in a series of articles which analyzed the impact of mechanization on the individual worker. He argued that in England a contemporary worker produced forty times more than he had prior to industrialization, but nevertheless, he was more likely now to lack the means of subsistence. Young Owen did not attack mechanization but the means of distribution and exchange. Warning against the encroaching impoverishment of the American worker, he endorsed the principle of collective ownership of the means of production and distribution as the appropriate alternative to capitalism. For the immediate future, he proposed government-owned storage areas such as would later be demanded by the Populists and other agrarian radicals.[22]

Most of young Owen's energy during his residence was absorbed by his work in the field of education, both as a teacher and writer. For his entire career as a reformer, Robert Dale Owen was committed to the belief that pedagogy was the basis of healthy change, both for the individual and for society at large. These views, originally shaped through his New Lanark boyhood and his Hofwyl education, were further expanded at New Harmony, and came to fruition later in New York where his ideas crystallized into a full program with political applications. For Robert Dale, a broad, practical, and meaningful education was the means for social regeneration. Suggestive of social engineering and intellectual manipulation, this perspective was shared by many pedagogical leaders of the nineteenth century.

When Robert Owen pronounced the preliminary society successful in January, 1826, a constitution for the newly christened New Harmony Community of Equals, embodying the new system, was promulgated. Robert Dale opposed the transformation as premature. He also argued against immediate membership in the community, suggesting at least a six-month period of probation. But the elder Owen's determination to complete his system prevailed.[23]

The new constitution proclaimed the community to be one family. A legislative assembly and an executive council were to govern. Through a hierarchy of officers, most of whom came from the inner circle of the preliminary society, the elder Owen's domination was assured. Economic equality was not established; while the constitution specified that real property would be placed in perpetual trust for the community, in fact Owen retained control and failed even to spell out the manner in which members could lease or purchase land. Full equality was still only a promise.

Morale soon collapsed. Scarcities intensified and physical conditions deteriorated. After a few weeks, the residents chose to cast aside all pretense of equality and requested that Owen assume full control and management of the community.[24] New Harmony as an experiment in cooperation and equality had failed. Within the year several dissolutions and reorganizations occurred and in the spring of 1827 the elder Owen left.

New Harmony had been handicapped at its origin by the weaknesses and mistakes of its founder. Owen, the absolute authority, had never settled basic questions as to property rights and community practices. Despite his original intentions, he had not selected the residents. His absence from New Harmony in its crucial organizational stage led to a haphazard, chaotic atmosphere that was never dispelled. The vacuum in leadership resulted in a noncohesive, heterogeneous group divided by class, religion, nationality, and ideals, and lacking a sense of direction. However, even if Owen had been present for the duration of the experiment, it is unlikely that the evolution of the community would have been different in outline. He was not a man for details and he frequently took a declaration for an implementation. Moreover, it has been questioned whether the United States was the appropriate scene for Owen's experiment. Although the young nation seemed a viable locale for innovation, Owen had no understanding of the distinct outlook, conditions, and other variables influencing the personalities and development of the American people. His whirlwind national tours did little to acquaint him with American society.[25]

Robert Dale Owen and William Owen judged that their father had minimized to a disastrous extent the background experiences of the residents. This was an ironic miscalculation since the determinant role of environment was the keystone of Owen's thought. "Our opinion is, that Robert Owen ascribed too little influence to the early, anti-social circumstances that had surrounded many of the quickly-collected inhabitants. . . ." they wrote. Before the dissolution Robert Dale had theorized in an unsigned editorial that even if the cooperative venture failed, the validity of the system would not be disproved. When the fact of failure could no longer be avoided, he expressed confidence in the theory of cooperative communities and its eventual fruition. At New Harmony measures had been premature, there had been no screening of potential residents, and the innumerable changes in organization during the last year had precluded the development of a sense of community among heterogeneous residents.[26]

Before New Harmony fragmented, Robert Dale Owen had already begun to disassociate himself from the community. Disappointed with the disparity between the theoretical and the practical, his residence only lasted sixteen months. Much later he would denigrate his youthful enthusiasms as indicative of an overdeveloped ". . . opinion of the good which I imagined that I could do, in the way of enlightening my fellow-creatures."[27] But at that time his discouragement had been brief and his energies were directed into new channels.

New Harmony, falling far short of its major goal, had many far-ranging sequels, some of which were related to its essential communitarian principle. One Scottish immigrant to the United States, an acquaintance of the Owen family, visited the colony and reflected upon its usefulness for the solution of a peculiar American problem. Frances Wright (1795-1852), a thirty-year-old Scotswoman, determined to adapt the main thrust of New Harmony to a plan of gradual emancipation of slaves, the success of which she hoped would serve as an example to the nation. Her effort to implement her program enjoyed the support and participation of several New Harmony communitarians, primarily Robert Dale Owen.

Frances Wright, the product of an aristocratic background leavened by liberal influences, had been impressed by the United

States during her visit in 1818-1819. The ostensible purpose of her tour was the promotion of her budding career as a playwright, but her fascination with the new nation as a beacon of liberty came to dominate her attention. Focusing on the opportunities she noted, and minimizing the inequalities, she was, unlike so many European visitors of the era delighted by everything. Upon her return to the United States in 1824, after exposure to English reformers and French republicans, she cast a somewhat more critical eye on the American scene. She was convinced that this new society, as Crèvecoeur had observed in the previous century, was creating a totally new individual. She resolved that his potential for growth must be harnessed to socially desirable ends.[28]

Frances Wright had been orphaned at an early age and, though reared by relatives, her basic situation led to self-reliance and a sense of independence. She was contemptuous of upper-class life, and insisted that the title due a fine lady was one she would gladly avoid. She claimed, however, that she shared with other young women of her background "a natural taste for retirement. . . ." But Frances Wright's commitments to egalitarianism, education, and environmental determinism, caused her to choose a public life. Her quest for equal rights for all implicitly focused attention on the role of women in liberal and industrial society, and she became one of the most renowned as well as vilified figures of her time.[29]

The basis of her reformism was her Lockean theory of knowledge. She believed that knowledge was attained via the senses from the natural world, and therefore was available to all human beings as long as their senses were not obstructed by false teachings of government or church. Once minds were unclouded and free to receive accurate sensations, human beings could introduce order and design into their environment. True knowledge, attained from matter, was the only guide through life.

Male and female, white and black, all were capable of perceptive inquiry and, therefore, of autonomy and equality. Once the ability of inquiry was released, ". . . universal improvement of our human condition. . ." would be realized She never doubted that peaceful change was possible and violent revolution unnecessary.[30]

Frances Wright was free of the racism that characterized so many nineteenth-century liberals, and yet she was so deeply convinced of the determinant role of environment that she assumed a paternalist posture toward people of color. It was not pigment that made the Indian and the African in America unqualified for citizenship, she wrote, but their exploitation by the white man. Their proximity to what she termed half-civilized white society meant the fostering of external vices rather than the promotion of moral and intellectual virtues. She recommended an apprenticeship for freedom, especially for the enslaved.[31]

She had no illusions about the rampant prejudices in all sections of the United States, and consequently, colonization after emancipation seemed to her the logical policy. However, she realized that the entire black population of the United States could not be colonized abroad, and hence she envisioned the eventual amalgamation of white and black as the soundest course. As a foreigner, Frances Wright was free of cultural taboos, and was able to offer dispassionate analyses that eluded many native-born Americans.[32]

She related the issue of the emancipation of the slaves to the status of the white working man. He also was subjugated, she thought, because of the social degradation associated with labor and because of his lack of education. The emancipation of the white laborer lay in worker unity and cooperation. She was convinced that cooperation rather than competition was advantageous to society. Possibly, she reasoned, cooperative labor and emancipation could be a single path to the goal of general happiness.[33]

The influences which played upon her and shaped her course of action were several. Through her contacts with the religious communitarians—Shakers and Rappites—and with nonsectarian English settlements,[34] Frances Wright was struck by the efficacy of communal efforts. From her friendship with Lafayette she was familiar with the details of his experiment with gradual emancipation a generation earlier on his plantation at Cayenne, French Guiana. She had toured the United States in 1825 with Lafayette and had visited the aging Thomas Jefferson and James Madison. In conversations with these men and with planters of lesser renown, she realized that many Southerners recognized slavery to be both immoral and unprofitable and were eager for a means of freeing themselves of its onus. Finally and most importantly, the New Harmony social system, with its stress on the significance of environment led her to sketch a new set of economic and social relationships which were to supersede the existing system.[35]

Late in 1825, a colony called Nashoba, the Chickasaw name for the nearby Wolf River, was founded on three hundred acres purchased by Frances Wright near Memphis, Tennessee. A handful of slaves was bought, transported to Nashoba and employed there to work their way to freedom through the profits of their labor. When capital investment and interest were met, emancipation and colonization would follow. It was presumed that other slaveholders would follow this inexpensive route out of slavery and that white free labor would move into the South to fill the vacuum left by the departure of thousands of Africans.[36]

Simplifying and paring down her original plan, Frances Wright reduced the number of personnel projected for the experiment and postponed for one year the establishment of an Owenite school to teach skills necessary for freedom. While she was somewhat contemptuous of emancipation societies for failing to educate the slaves for full freedom, she felt that the overwhelming dimensions of the experiment in the wilderness prohibited any but essential tasks. A few whites from New Harmony managed the small plantation under her watchful eye until after a few months malaria, contracted through exertion and exposure, forced her to retire from her supervisory role. She placed Nashoba and her other property in trust for her slaves in the event of her death.[37]

In the summer of 1826 Frances Wright visited New Harmony once again, and thereafter she decided to impose a new social structure on the plantation. Nashoba was henceforth to serve as a communitarian colony for a white elite while it continued as an experiment in emancipation. Because the conveniently available slaves would do the heavy tasks, the whites accepted for membership could contribute either labor or funds to Nashoba, while enjoying one another's "morally cultivated" companionship in "lettered leisure."[38] An integrated school for the white and black children at Nashoba would contribute in the long run to undermining social polarization. The plan was attractive enough to captivate trustee Robert Dale Owen as a settler. After ten days, however, the partially cleared land, mosquito-infested and infertile, and the few squalid cabins, totally lacking the barest civilized amenities, convinced him that his own tastes could be better satisfied by escorting Frances Wright on the sea voyage which her poor health required.[39]

While the two were abroad, the trustee in charge, James Richardson, a free-thinking Scotsman, proudly published news of Nashoba, including his own liaison with one of the slaves. This scandalous information, as well as the benevolently despotic treatment of the slaves as revealed in the publication, turned both advanced and mass opinion against the Nashoba experiment. While Frances Wright hastily composed some "explanatory notes," she felt devastated. If others could so lightly play with the fate of the people to whose cause she was committed, it became "... a hopeless task to venture ought for suffering humanity. What we want ... is a few of elevated sentiment who will say 'I take my stand for the cause and not for myself.'..."[40] But Nashoba was now vilified as an interracial brothel, and the remaining stabs at its resurrection failed. A few years later she accompanied her slaves to Haiti and freedom. To the end she believed that their best interest lay in education and freedom elsewhere.

Several years later Frances Wright wrote that the whole experiment had been an error, that it had been too ambitious for a few individuals, however dedicated. Only a collective and unified effort could have effected basic improvements in the human condition. Had Frances Wright analyzed Nashoba in greater detail, she might well have concluded that under any circumstances its chances were nil. She and a handful of colleagues sought to build a colony in the wilderness as had many religious communities; they attempted to educate slaves for freedom as a few others had tried to do; and they sought to impose a new social order which was already failing at New Harmony. Seldom had so few attempted so much. While her biographer maintains that her serious error consisted of succumbing to New Harmony radicalization, Nashoba was headed for disaster even before that fatal step.[41]

Frances Wright, however, was not defeated. She immediately turned to her other reform interests, such as the labor movement, public education, and women's rights. Her career as a lecturer in the public arena will be dealt with later.

Possibly the most noteworthy among other communitarian experiments conducted by newcomers was Etienne Cabet's "Icarie." Cabet, a French lawyer (1788-1856), whose own background included Carbonari conspiracies and the July Revolution of 1830, composed a romantic novel entitled *Voyage en Icarie*. His descriptions of a new system of social organization based on complete equality won Cabet a wide following among the French. At a time when France endured both the lassitude of Louis Philippe's July Monarchy and the alienation of early industrialism, the utopia pictured by the French lawyer was pieced together out of the writings of earlier social analysts such as Sir Thomas More and Bonnet de Mably. It captivated its readers. Indeed, Cabet found himself under pressure to organize an Icarian community as an example to the French nation.[42]

Cabet, who had been exposed to Owenite influences during five years of English exile as an anti-monarchist conspirator, envisioned republican government resting on participatory democracy and common property rights. Based on his beliefs in man's perfectibility and his god-given right to happiness, Cabet postulated that superior social and political organization would result in fraternity, equality, and liberty. Under communism, all citizens would know complete equality, would operate collectively the means of production and distribution, and would have available to them a full range of social services. They would live as separate families sharing common facilities within self-sufficient communes of limited size. Each citizen would exercise self-government through his commune officials, whom he could recall at will. A similar system of representation would prevail on the provincial and national levels. With the exception of Cabet's espousal of early Christianity, it was Owen's stamp that rested upon him.[43]

Three groups of would-be Icarians traveled to the United States in 1848 and 1849, heading for land which Cabet had arranged to purchase adjacent to the Red River in Texas. The eruption of the February Revolution in Paris reduced their number to at most five hundred. Predictably, these determined pioneers were defeated by Texas climate and disease, the wilderness conditions, and the deception of the land agent who had sold Cabet noncontiguous acreage. They finally settled in Nauvoo, Illinois, in March, 1849, purchasing homes and property from the recently banished Mormon community. Quickly establishing themselves, they prospered as a self-sustaining community of farmers and craftsmen embodying the Protestant ethic. Icaria combined individual property ownership with economic planning, social equality, and a communal life style. The political framework, unlike the economic, more nearly epitomized original expectations as an annually elected Board of Directors, led by Cabet, administered the community's affairs in concert with a legislative body of all male adults. Democracy flourished with full communism as a future goal.[44]

For a half dozen years the Icarians seemed to thrive on the Illinois prairie. However, conflict over constitutional revisions erupted in 1855, resulting in the breakup of the community.

Cabet and his loyalists, a minority, were expelled, and whatever strategy they mapped out for a return expired with Cabet's sudden death in St. Louis in 1856. Until the end of the century, with changes of locale and division of personnel, various Icarias existed in the Old Northwest, but the communist experiment remained unrealized. Whether responsibility for the Nauvoo fiasco lay with an increasingly dictatorial Cabet, incapable of loosening the reins on his own creation, or whether the growing material success of the residents provoked friction and jealousy, Icaria was realized most perfectly in its fictionized version.[45]

In addition to Robert Owen, the other influential European in secular communitarianism in the United States was Charles Fourier (1772-1827). In the eighteen-forties a movement labeled "associationism" blossomed. Various communities were organized under the principles of Fourier, and they attracted native Americans, especially the New England elite. Immigrant radicals played little part in the movement. Fourierism was adopted, shaped, and introduced to the United States by one of the first Americans to be a product of a European education. Albert Brisbane (1809-1890) was himself as much shaped by Europe as by his indigenous American roots, and he sought to impose a European-conceived school of thought upon Americans.

Brisbane's belief that the United States mistakenly clung to old institutions despite economic and social transformation, led him to seize upon Fourierism as a demonstration that human labor could be reorganized on a basis of dignity. He endorsed communities or phalanxes of 1,800 people living in association and also endorsed the idea of cooperative production.[46]

After Brisbane's several years of study abroad, he returned to his New York State home in 1834 and soon thereafter turned his attention to propaganda. Only one Fourierist society existed at that time, composed of French émigrés and a few Americans. Brisbane addressed his propaganda and translations of Fourier to Americans, whom he informed that Fourierism was not an imported novelty but "the culminating expression of all social ideals that have built the American republic."⁴⁷ Any other reform, whether emancipation or female suffrage, would leave the deep sources of social discontent untouched, he said. Brisbane's writings were sufficient to attract the attention of a number of discontented American intellectuals. Ultimately about forty communities were organized, the most famous of which was the ill-fated Brook Farm of the New England Transcendentalists. The majority had no direct experience with industrial conditions but, rather, represented middle-class resentment, discontent, and criticism of American society. Each phalanx was no more than a fleeting moment of protest.⁴⁸

The nineteenth century communitarian movement in all of its various guises came to an end at mid-century. By that time economic conditions did not favor the organization of such communities. The initial expenses of procuring necessities made such experiments unfeasible. Intellectual currents honed on the actual experience of hard-won knowledge also opposed further experimentation. The artificiality of a communal society created overnight not only had a slight chance for longevity but it also lacked any relation to the larger society, as beacon or example. Only religious communitarians, because of their cohesiveness, had shown a tendency toward permanence.

However, the secular enterprises, individualistic to the core, demonstrated a striking tendency to collapse after a short interlude of collective goodwill and joint effort. But these secular communitarians served a purpose in American history: they shaped the communitarian tradition in its last days away from its religious orientation and toward social awareness. When their communities failed to thrive, they formed grist for the mill of industrial society's oncoming problems as some of them turned to gradualist reformism.⁴⁹

Labor Activists

In the Jacksonian Era, men of British origin were involved in the nascent labor movement and they played a special part in the drama. Englishmen, Scots, and Welsh generally emigrated to the United States for material advancement, as did others, but these immigrants did not come empty-handed. Because their motherland had pioneered in industrialization, these immigrants had the background and the experience that tended to equip them for the changing American economy, in contrast to the majority of immigrants whose background was agrarian. Many from the British Isles (the exception, of course, were the immigrants from underdeveloped and impoverished Ireland) brought with them crafts and skills which allowed them to move into specific trades and, indeed, to transform those developing industries. For those who came without particular training there was at least familiarity with industrial society and with the tools of literacy (common despite the scarcity of formal elementary schooling in England). Therefore they were able to adapt easily and avail themselves of whatever opportunities they found.[50]

The British domination of the early decades of American industrialization, enduring until indigenous technology took over and discarded Old World models, had various implications. The unique perspectives of these "Anglo-Americans," men of two cultures, meant that they imposed alien evaluations upon American conditions and that their judgments would undergo modification and even transformation.

The labor movement of the third and fourth decade of the nineteenth century was a response to the weakened bargaining power of the workers as a result of early mechanization. Workers in all trades (with the exception of factory operatives who tended to be women and children) joined with sympathizers to protest eloquently against their growing insecurity in the face of the decreasing importance of skills.[51] The British immigrants endowed the movement with their own particular coloring. These workers were accustomed to a distinctive framework: they thought in terms of rights and responsibilities they shared as a class. If a right were threatened, they must defend that right as a class. If a response, either defensive or offensive, were required, that response ought properly to be a collective one. Unlike so many native Americans, these immigrants knew how to act in groups. They saw their struggle for existence in terms of their group or class identity.

Thus, these British immigrants combined vital industrial skills with a class perspective. To employers they were both indispensable and irritating. Consequently, British immigrants played a not surprisingly major role in the early labor movement, both as participants and leaders. As agitators, orators, editors, spokesmen, and, later, organizers, they shaped principles and techniques and heightened the level of awareness among American workers. While they alone were not the catalysts of the labor movement, their role was important in shaping it.[52]

Those British immigrants who assumed leadership in the American labor movement originated from every part of the social spectrum, ranging from workingmen supporting themselves by plying a trade to small capitalists and wealthy dabblers in reforms. To some, their efforts in the labor movement brought them the only prominence they would ever know, while for others participation was no more than a fleeting episode in a lengthy public career.

William Heighton (1800-1873) was a Philadelphia cordwainer whose *Mechanics' Free Press* was the first American newspaper to be edited for and by journeymen. Heighton, who appears to have come to the United States from England in childhood, practiced his trade until the organization of the Mechanics' Union of Trade Associations in 1827. Through the *Free Press* this relatively "unlettered mechanic," as he styled himself, led the workers of his county in their unionist and political activities.

The basis of Heighton's thought was the conviction that producers must receive the full fruits of their labor. While the only student of Heighton's career has likened his ideas to those of the Ricardian socialists,[53] consideration of Heighton's life suggests that his philosophy was shaped on the anvil of experience; its similarity to that of John Gray, a Scottish Ricardian economist whom he read, appears less due to intellectual inspiration than to direct observations and deductions during the years spent in the craftshops of the City of Brotherly Love. In the company of others who worked with their hands, Heighton saw men denied an adequate share of the wealth they created. He blamed the government for failing to promote the general welfare. In Heighton's judgment, legislators catered to the nonproducers, an inexcusable policy for a government dedicated to promoting equality.

The solution Heighton espoused was that the workers educate one another through newspapers, libraries, and societies, and then utilize their suffrage to elect their own representatives. If workers understood the dimensions of the emergent industrial system, he averred, they would avoid temptations of irrelevant communitarian schemes and, rather, seek to control the existing economic order for their own benefit. The largely unarticulated socialism of William Heighton made him somewhat impatient with the bread-and-butter, hours-and-wages approach of the Mechanics' Union. In the face of its first and fatal disappointing experience at the polls in November, 1828, Heighton's indifference to the immediate outcome was clear. His only concern was that Philadelphia's workers be roused sufficiently from their inertia to insure the founding of a workers' party.[54] His personal disappointment in the next year over the end of the movement must have been profound, yet somewhat alleviated by signs of imitation in the other industrial states.

In 1835 another transplanted Englishman began the publication of a Philadelphia weekly devoted to the interests of the workingmen. Thomas Brothers (1800-18?) was an anomaly in the early labor movement in that he was a manufacturer employing several journeymen. Brothers lived in the United States for fourteen years before returning to England in 1838 in disillusionment. For this immigrant from the British Isles, then, the American experience was only a relatively brief interlude; England served as the framework for his career and, indeed, for his views throughout his life.

Brothers emigrated in order to improve his financial position as a small manufacturer and, secondly, in order to enjoy the blessings of representative government. He admired the young nation as it moved toward unrestricted suffrage. However, he appears to have held ambiguous views on the subject of self-government, considering it no more than an experiment, and he was never certain that "... the people in mass ..." were in fact capable of sovereignty. His readings in England of Thomas Paine, and possibly also of William Cobbett, both of whom he later rejected, had taught him the helplessness of the dispossessed. They had also convinced him that economic oppression was the handmaiden of the industrial and commercial developments he had witnessed. The tirades of Tom Paine against the national debt unjustly burdening the masses, and Cobbett's attacks on paper money as a fraud perpetuated upon the people, were echoed at various times in Brothers's writings on monetary reforms.[55]

In his small business, he struggled against what he termed the usurping, commercial aristocracy. He began to denounce the "interlocking conspiracy" of swindling politicians, greedy monopolists, and specie manipulators. From his own increasing bitterness as well as because of genuine sympathy for the workingmen whom he considered equally victimized, Brothers participated in the revival of the Philadelphia labor movement over the ten-hour day in 1835. He was active as editor and publisher of the *Radical Reformer and Working Man's Advocate* and as public speaker. While some workers apparently resented the participation of this employer, "He saw no irony in the advice he continually gave workingmen, that to secure their objectives they should depend on their own efforts alone and reject the aid proffered by well-meaning employers."[56] Brothers's attacks on capitalism intensified as did his assaults on the workings of the system of representative government. He particularly attacked the program of internal improvements which appeared to be no more than a bottomless pork barrel and which, he wrote, demonstrated no sign of easing the people's burdens. The incessant granting of charters to the rich and the mortgaging of the country's future through debt were constantly criticized in the pages of his weekly. Brothers came to believe suffrage to be worthless, for the people neither protected themselves through it nor were they protected by so-called representative institutions.[57]

Thomas Brothers experienced financial ruin in the Panic of 1837, after which he returned to England. Brothers had lost both his fortune and his youthful ideals: his business had failed, the workers had rejected his leadership, and, he believed, the country itself had proven unfaithful to its own, albeit misguided, values. His reflections on his experiences emphasized the social problems in the United States, American intolerance of differences, and especially the ignorance of the mob. His fears of the possibility that a demagogic-inspired violence might bring about a French-style American Revolution led him to favor limited suffrage and government by aristocratic elements. Indeed, even the idea of an enlightened despot had an attraction for him, for "... would it not be better to live under him, than under a miserable cheating designing set of creatures ... ?" Self-government had meant anarchy and, hence, property-based elitist rule became his standard as he was "... once more safe in 'Old England.'"[58]

In New York City a transplanted Englishman assumed a major role in the political awakening of the workingmen. To understand the twisted path taken by the workingman's movement there, it is perhaps best to trace its history through the career of the most visible and most ubiquitous of its leaders—George Henry Evans—who edited the *Working Man's Advocate* and fifteen years later compiled the only history of the movement by a participant. A partial explanation for the meandering policy may be attributable to Evans's impressionability and his own acceptance of a variety of programs.[59]

George Henry Evans (1805-1856) had arrived on these shores as a lad seeking a trade. His widowed father apprenticed George to a printer and his brother Frederick to a hatter; the elder Evans, somewhat accustomed to the amenities of life through his marriage into the English landed gentry, was anxious to provide his sons with a good foundation for life's struggles.

This immigrant from rural Herefordshire spent a lifetime embracing one reform after another as he sought a path that would lead American workers away from industrial alienation. Evans was almost unique among reformers; he was a good-natured and tolerant activist who was capable of rational debate totally devoid of personal assaults. A plain man, he knew both the world of the print shop and the world of the printed word, and consequently his familiarity with each allowed him to straddle barriers that other reformers could not. He would no more restrict shopowners from the workingmen's political movement than he would exclude mechanics from his debating society; he had seen at firsthand the trials and the despair of each. In taking the route from a lower-middle-class upbringing to leadership of workers and land reformers, he was nourished by Old World intellectual wellsprings as he focused on New World developments and possibilities. Always the champion of the workingman who was to him the embodiment of the hope of America, "... he was so naturally imbued with the spirit of democracy that he brought it to bear on every question he discussed."[60]

Evans appears to have been introduced by his father to the teachings of Thomas Spence, the eighteenth-century English agrarian. Spence taught that property should be owned collectively through a series of national communes which would rent the land to cultivators and use the rentals to cover governmental expenditures. Such communal ownership of the land within the context of a skeletal government would insure egalitarian conditions. Evans's acceptance of the necessity of having land available to everyone approached Spence's projected social and political reformation, while his stress on granting land to cultivators without charge outdistanced Spence's agrarianism. While Evans intermittently chased after other panaceas, he always returned to his agrarian theme and it was the framework of his career.[61]

According to the autobiography of his brother, a leader of the

Shaker community, another influence on Evans was Thomas Paine. Both boys read Paine, with the result that George Henry Evans was a lifelong atheist, a fact he often minimized in his propaganda. He deliberately avoided religious issues, even though he regarded the organized church as an enemy of the workingman.[62] Clearly, Evans's intellectual convictions were molded by his readings. But, as in the case of William Heighton, his experiences as a workingman no doubt shaped him most decisively and prepared him for his entry into the workers' movement when he moved to Manhattan from upstate New York in 1829.[63]

Evans could be found everywhere. He chaired workers' meetings, he helped sponsor Robert Dale Owen's "New York Association for the Protection of Industry and for the Promotion of National Education," he founded a political debating society for the local workers, and even occasionally stood as a candidate for public office. His indefatigable writings, under the proud phrase "edited by a mechanic," touched all social and political issues. He confronted what he called the useless classes, composed of lawyers, bankers, and clergymen, while encouraging those he considered useful. He reproduced excerpts from *Cobbett's Register* and alerted his readers to English unionization attempts. He encouraged the efforts of women operatives and invited others to support them; he congratulated New York black men for calling the attention of the legislators to their lack of suffrage; and he welcomed political refugees to the United States.[64] At various times, he favored workers' candidates for public office, either in their own right or in order to bring pressure on Tammany Hall. He supported a national trade union, and even combined the political and economic aims of labor by endorsing the idea of political unions independent of existing political parties.[65]

New York City workers first met in the spring of 1829 for the purpose of retaining the ten-hour day, then under attack by employers. After it appeared that worker mobilization had secured that objective, attention was transferred to political grievances. They demanded equal land for all at the age of maturity, endorsing a resolution which proclaimed man's natural rights to the land. To win that goal, candidates were named for November state elections, and Ebenezer Ford, a carpenter, was elected to the State Assembly of New York; some of their other candidates approached victory, and the workingmen won over one-third of the ballots cast.[66]

Enthusiasm after the strong showing was followed by quarrels over party structure and policy. By the end of the year a schism occurred as the native leader, Thomas Skidmore, and his closest followers founded a new, still-born organization dedicated to agrarianism and confined in membership to bona fide workers.[67] The next year there were three separate parties claiming to be the original, with the Evans group probably containing its nucleus.

The policy differences which shredded the party were reflected in the turn from agrarianism to a national system of free education, personified by Evans's change of heart.[68] Whereas Evans's original acceptance of the agrarian resolutions had been unqualified, he quickly reversed himself. To whatever extent he had accepted land reformism, by the time of the election he was arguing against property redistribution as a means to the achievement of fundamental social justice. He had become convinced that equal distribution of property would be overturned within a year. Unequal wealth would prevail, despite legislative manipulation, so long as workers were denied opportunities for education. Unequal education was "the most injurious species of inequality" and only equal education would effectively remedy social ills.[69]

However, Evans was somewhat less than sanguine about the total efficacy of free education and housing at government expense. He indicated that if the implementation of conditions of equality, including educational opportunities, resulted in fresh inequities, he would accept the new situation as a natural development.

Modifications of the plan did not save the rump-party as a

new split occurred late in the spring. By the time of the August state convention of New York workers' parties, the New York City party had fragmented unrecognizably.[70]

Evans helped to bring about a resurgence of the working-men's movement in New York City in the middle 1830's, and then he retired temporarily. Ill and bankrupt, he lived as a farmer in New Jersey. Six years later, when he returned to his life as a printer and agitator in New York, he called the alienation of man from the soil the most fundamental source of injustice in Western civilization. Had Evans been aware of it, the Marxist stress on man's alienation from the tools of production probably would have seemed to him no more than a byproduct of denial of access to the land. To Evans, a republic which did not provide access to the soil for all citizens violated the principle of popular sovereignty. While Evans denied that he favored a forced redistribution of land, he did insist that title should be awarded on the basis of use rather than purchase. He argued that a responsible Congress must make acreage available to the landless. Every other reform, no matter how desirable, was to him subordinate to the goal of free soil to settlers. In his revived *Working Man's Advocate*, he invited the support of Fourierists, trade unionists, temperance workers, peace advocates, and abolitionists for his National Reform Association's effort to terminate "slavery" of every type.[71]

With the support of several disciples Evans widely publicized his theories on agrarianism. He favored the granting of one hundred and sixty acres with free lifetime tenure to potential farmers. Settlers could sell only their improvements on the land. In some ways, Evans's plan has been said to foreshadow the Homestead Act of 1862. But that act lacked his inheritance and sales restrictions geared to create an economically and politically sovereign class of yeoman farmers. The Homestead Act was unrelated to Evans's dream of neighboring farms composing

township democracies, where all could meet in proper person and vote directly for laws and judicature [sic], without the intervention of officers, as well as to have the power of self-employment upon their own homesteads without that of landlords.[72]

Evans did not pioneer the concept of free homesteads, but he helped transfer the idea from the realm of charity to that of natural rights.[73]

To generalize on the goals of American working people from the 1820's to the 1840's might be a pointless task, for a list of various planks culled from the platforms of different parties and programs would indicate that organized workingmen aspired mainly to gaining advantages enjoyed by other Americans. But, in addition, they pursued some goals which applied only to working men and women.

As an example of the latter point, the workingmen's party of New York in its first year demanded an end to imprisonment for debts and to convict-labor competition, abolition of or revision of the militia system, an effective lien law, a less expensive judicial system, and a national system of education. Farther afield, workers also called for the abolition of licensed monopolies, the implementation of equal taxation of property, and of a district system of elections, and a separation of church and state. As the John R. Commons classic study concluded, "In general, the workingmen of this period were ardent champions of all reforms, . . ."[74]

Superimposed on these specifics that were hammered into countless programs were ideological assumptions and statements. The influence of the English-born leaders seems particularly clear in the willingness of the workingmen to act as groups in opposition to powerful, hostile forces. They, joined by some native-born leaders, convinced workers that individual action invited defeat, and they led the workers in their first strong efforts at solidarity. Thus they can be said to have given birth to the American labor movement. However, to demonstrate collective action is not to prove that class cohesiveness or even a firm sense of class consciousness existed. The fact remains that both leaders and rank and file in the labor movement did not see themselves as permanent members of the working class. While they might struggle to help one another, they did not tend to consider themselves fixed in their social status or economic scale. An exhaustive biographical study of the leaders of New York workingmen in the 1830's concludes that ambition, vitality, even mobility, characterized their careers and their life styles.[75] These were men who did not intend to stay in places assigned to them by life's accidents. Unlike England, the United States did not, as far as they were concerned, impose traditional and permanent status. The existence of a working class was a fact of life, but its membership, they wished to believe, was fluid.

A second assumption emphasized by the men who stood on the soapboxes and the speaker's platforms was the necessity of modifying the free enterprise system. Their implicit anticapitalism often assumed the form of an undefined socialism as they, from their various perspectives as cordwainers, printers, or wealthy sympathizers, stressed the injustice of the producers of wealth receiving less than their share. The pursuit of social, economic, and political justice and equality were the constant themes of leaders, whether they stressed land, monetary, or educational reforms. They tended not to spell out the dimensions of their ideal society and, for the most part, refrained from advocating revolution.[76] However, inherent in their various plans was a differently structured society, with a focus on social responsibility, a cohesive community, and individual opportunity within a collective framework. The blatant element in their thought was the stress on the collective in a country noted for its emphasis on the individual. In this fundamental regard it can be argued that the leadership did not relate to the rank and file because "this new man, the American" had had his consciousness shaped and his institutions geared to capitalist ideology for two hundred years. At a time when each man, pursuing upward mobility, could imagine one day opening a shop or farming his own homestead, there was little chance that he would reject basic postulates in favor of a new system in which he might enjoy collective security. The implicit socialist orientation of the leadership was unlikely to have been acceptable to the movement as a whole.

The goals most heavily underlined at various times by the workingman's movement were education and agrarianism. Each of these programs, in a different guise, eventually entered the general consciousness and became reality, with the public school systems established in the various states and the Homestead Act of 1862. As originally conceived, these goals were regarded as the means by which to transform American society into a truly egalitarian system. The rank and file may or may not have understood the implications of the declaration that all men have an inalienable right to the soil; they may have pinned all their hopes to republican education to save the future generation or their acceptance of that goal may have been exaggerated by enemies of the movement in order to cause dissension and disruption, but labor clearly played a vital role in creating a climate of acceptance for these reforms.

While workingmen may have been content with reforming the militia system and obtaining a lien law and other direct benefits, they also served as catalysts in moving the government to accept responsibility toward the securing of goals which thus far had been pursued haphazardly. To what extent the organized workingmen accepted the assumptions and theories of the leadership is not clear and may never be, but what is manifest —and has never been adequately stressed—is the significant role played by those leaders of English birth.

These men imposed their larger perspectives, developed programs based on those views, strengthened the sense of class consciousness and, as has recently been noted, reinforced a perhaps weakening belief in the Republic's ability to solve its problems. Lacking the desperate sense of alienation which characterized the revolutionaries living in autocratic systems, "Britons demonstrated by peaceful methods labor could go far toward achieving its goals, even alter the complexion of government without smashing existing institutions."[77] The role these immigrant radicals played was crucial to the early labor movement and to the American Republic inasmuch as it delayed its violent industrial phase.

Immigrant Feminists

Among the various efforts to encourage political and social change in the antebellum United States, it was the female emancipation movement which drew almost exclusively upon native personnel. As recent studies argue, it grew out of needs and demands of middle-class American women for autonomy and independence.[78] Within the framework of middle-class values, those women who felt that their individuality was stifled by a lack of opportunity, banded together in order to win recognition of their own right to full participation in national life. The alteration in the status quo which they sought was not so much social as it was personal, not so much structural as it was psychological.

Three immigrant feminists played noteworthy but historically neglected roles in the movement, and served both to broaden its scope and perspective and to universalize its meaning. One was the Scotswoman Frances Wright, already discussed as a communitarian and emancipator, who may be considered a forerunner of the organized feminist movement. The other two were the Polish-born Ernestine Potowski Rose and the Westphalian Forty-eighter Mathilde Franziska Giesler-Anneke. All three shared values and ideologies that transcended those of the native feminists, and all of them posed basic challenges to the social, economic, and political framework of their adopted nation.

These three radical personalities were freethinkers who (each in her own way) were rebels against Metternichean Europe and brought to the United States a commitment to a rational reordering of social processes. Each was independent in spirit and in fact. All of them were educated, literary women who enjoyed the personal autonomy and self-confidence for which the American-born feminists fought. Frances Wright and Madame Anneke had the strength and self-assurance which sometimes result from an aristocratic upbringing in a tightly drawn class system, while

Mrs. Rose had the insights and determination derived from life as a marginal person—a Jew in Christian Central Europe.

These three feminists were unafraid to question fundamentals, whether they were of a religious or of a political nature. They demanded social restructuring, not because it would mean their own emancipation, but because they believed that social justice and individual fulfillment required that society become rational. All three women had sufficient sense of self to transcend issues of personal identity. They were free of middle-class values and hence proceeded to redefine roles, responsibilities, institutions, and even mores. Their views in some areas were so advanced that their challenges were not only unheeded but scorned. Nevertheless, they added a profound dimension to the American feminist movement.

Frances Wright epitomized in her own personality and career the emancipated woman. Her devotion to the ideal of a reasonably ordered society inevitably focused attention on the status of her sex. As the pioneer among female public lecturers, she invited catcalls, mob scenes, and even the necessity of bodyguards by merely ascending the public rostrum. She persevered despite such dangers because her first experiences as a social reformer had convinced her that the popular mind must be enlightened before social experimentation had any chance of success.[79]

On the platform she made a striking impression: tall and straight, simply dressed, with an attractive but solemn demeanor. Strength and resolution shone through, and for the sympathetic, such as her friend, Frances Trollope, "... all ... expectations fell far short of the splendour, the brillance [*sic*], the overwhelming eloquence of this extraordinary orator."[80] On the other hand, for the hostile, it was as if Lucifer himself were responsible for such a public performer. A former mayor of New York City, Philip Hone, attacked her as "a female Tom Paine" who "would unsettle the foundations of civil society." Frances Wright consoled herself that "...though the ...enemy may hunt me from house to house...." the breaching of the walls of ignorance was worth any sacrifice she was forced to make.[81]

Her experiences with unfriendly crowds and locked lecture halls resulted from her topics as well as her very appearance. While she lectured on slave emancipation, mass education, and workingmen's political parties, as did other public figures, she also addressed herself to the role of women in American society, their legal and sexual interests, including marriage, divorce, and even birth control. She frequently singled out organized religion for attack, particularly in its political manifestations and in its effects on American women. The predictable result was the charge of infidelism.[82]

To the friendly and antagonistic alike, Frances Wright came to personify the issue of the role of women in Jacksonian America. On women's rights, she wrote that

. . . until women assume the place in society which good sense and good feeling alike assign to them, human improvement must advance but feebly. It is in vain that we would circumscribe the power of one-half of our race, and that half by far the most important and influential. If they exert it not for good, they will for evil; if they advance not knowledge, they will perpetuate ignorance.[83]

She never asserted female superiority. Her concern was with the role women played as shapers of the future generations. No matter how limited their rights to property or their opportunities for education, they nevertheless were the dominant force in childrearing and so, Frances Wright argued, if only a portion of the younger generation could be enlightened, it must be the female contingent.[84]

She looked upon the entire legal system as coercive, whether in regard to white workingmen, to the enslaved, or to women. Her explanation for what appeared to her to be the anomaly of legal injustice was that the republican United States had assumed the common law of monarchical England, without the American public realizing its limitations. She used the English law particularly to illustrate the married woman's legal subordination. The "civil death" to which Sir William Blackstone sentenced women upon their marriages sharply curtailed their property and other rights. Frances Wright demanded nothing short of the legal resurrection of women.[85]

Her views of marriage and the family, based on her rationalism and skepticism, led to the most slanderous of the attacks upon her. Frances Wright viewed marriage as a personal arrangement, totally external to the state. Human relationships must not be legislated, she argued, for even if men and women were to favor legal vows, that very act itself would be harmful to those involved: legal obligations only weakened moral responsibility and sanctioned brutality. She did not believe that a ceremony could guarantee a permanent tie and, as long as the institution of marriage persisted—assuming it to be for the duration of man's unenlightened state—she favored the availability of divorce. Divorce seemed to her the rational and moral alternative when the parties had grown away from one another; moreover, the protection of children from a strife-torn atmosphere demanded it.[86]

She denounced the legal and social system for the ostracism to which children born out of wedlock were subjected and for the contempt in which the multiplying impoverished were held. She argued on behalf of her friend Robert Dale Owen's plan for state protection of children through a system of public boarding schools, and she recommended the utilization of birth control measures. Her endorsement of sexual emancipation shocked even some of her colleagues in reform. But at least Robert Dale Owen supported most of her positions, as witnessed by his pamphlet *Moral Physiology*, the first, and therefore notorious, birth control tract in the United States.[87]

Whatever success Frances Wright might have had in opening society to greater participation by women foundered on her sexual audacity. To pose this kind of challenge before a society is ready for it is to obscure every other issue and to insure defeat. While Frances Wright's public career paved the way for later feminist reformers, her positive impact at the time was nevertheless limited. Her ill-fated marriage, contracted in 1831 to the Frenchman William Phiquepal d'Arusmont, a former teacher at New Harmony, ironically foundered on his conception of the proper spheres of the two sexes, and resulted in divorce and d'Arusmont's rearing their only daughter to be an anti-feminist.

Ernestine Potowski Rose (1810-1892) was another early nine-teenth-century immigrant feminist whose inspiration was the Enlightenment and its egalitarianism. She was even a more precocious rebel than Frances Wright, for as an adolescent she had critically assessed the civilization of Russian-controlled Poland and judged its inadequacies. By the age of fourteen she was skeptical of the Jewish traditions within which she was reared; at sixteen she successfully challenged her widowed father's legal and moral right to shape her future through a betrothal of his choice; and at seventeen she left home. She spent the years between 1828 and 1831 traveling on the continent, supported only by her ingenuity. In those years she absorbed revolutionary currents which intensified her earlier hostility to oppression. Settling in England, she at once came under the spell of Robert Owen, and his views thereafter served as the underpinning of her moral outrage. By the time she came to the New World with her young English husband in 1836, she was a confirmed freethinker, a fiery orator, and a passionate reformer.[88]

Every aspect of her career and personality was the antithesis of the pattern to which she might have conformed. Each of the roles with which she was identified, a woman, an immigrant, a Pole, and a Jew, dictated subservience. Her unwillingness to fit into her niche invited considerable antagonism, and the hostility demonstrated against her sometimes rivaled that experienced by Frances Wright earlier.[89] Her special efforts were devoted to sexual and racial emancipation. She joined native middle-class women in the early period of the organized woman's rights movement, addressing various national and state conventions annually. On the legislative level, she led a successful twelve-year struggle for a married women's property bill in New York State. As an abolitionist, she was active throughout the country, including one foray in which she spoke alone and unprotected in Charleston, South Carolina, and she won recognition for extraordinary contributions to the cause by Wendell Phillips and others.[90]

Mrs. Rose lectured from Massachusetts to Michigan, and from New York to the South. Her lectures dealt with women's rights, social evils, religion, free public education, government, and socialism. Her husband's income as a craftsman was utilized to finance her tours, and only occasional ill health kept her from the lecture circuit.[91] Once on the platform, she was able to captivate all but the most hostile listeners, despite her foreign accent and her slight lisp. Her contagious enthusiasm, her incisive mind, and her ability to seize upon the crucial point in any argument not only persuaded an audience but steered her colleagues away from unimportant issues. Following the passage of the married women's property bill, she publicly proclaimed its limited application and suggested further reforms. She pointed out to the Women's Rights Convention in 1851, that at best the new legislation in New York meant some advances for the favored few. "... but for the laboring many, there is none."[92]

After the Civil War, she and her husband returned to England, and the last twenty-three years of her life were spent in furthering her ideals in an environment ranging between the egalitarian promises of the New World and the inflexible practices of her homeland. England served as the framework for her career in organized reform movements.

In 1853 Mrs. Rose helped to introduce to the woman's rights movement Mathilde Franziska Giesler-Anneke (1817-1884), for whom she had translated at a women's convention in New York. Prior to her debut in the organized movement, Madame Anneke had already devoted her adult life to struggle in the name of liberty and revolution. In her view, female emancipation was simply one battleground in a comprehensive struggle for freedom. Just as her predecessor, Mrs. Rose, had recognized that rights won for middle-class women left the masses of women unaffected, so Madame Anneke maintained that the emancipation of labor as a class would be incomplete without female emancipation.[93] Her views leaned toward a total reconstruction of society and this attitude placed her in a unique position in the movement for women's rights.

Mathilde Franziska Giesler had come from a prosperous background in Westphalia. Originally enjoying wealth and education, her carefree attitude toward life was disrupted by an early and unhappy marriage. By the age of twenty-one she had had an annulment, an infant daughter and, as a result of her struggle to maintain guardianship over her child, had developed a fierce determination to overturn injustice and inequities of all sorts. In 1847, she married Fritz Anneke, a Prussian military officer, whose radical orientation completed her own intellectual development from devout Catholicism to sweeping rationalism. They immersed themselves in radical circles in Cologne and published revolutionist newspapers, including her *Frauenzeitung*, the first nineteenth-century newspaper to stand for equal rights and full employment opportunities for women. Upon the eruption of the German Revolution in 1848, the Annekes participated in political and military events, and finally fled to Switzerland. In 1849 they emigrated to the United States.[94]

The Annekes settled in Wisconsin, drawn there by the large German community. While Fritz Anneke followed an unsuccessful journalistic career in various parts of the country, Madame Anneke pursued her own literary and lecturing endeavors in Milwaukee. After spending the years of the Civil War in Europe, she founded a school for girls.

Madame Anneke's fight for women's rights won few laurels in her own community. German spokesmen ridiculed her efforts and her *Deutsche Frauenzeitung* led a precarious existence. As dramatic evidence both of her commitment and of the obstacles she faced, a German printers' union prevented Madame Anneke from hiring women as typesetters. Her public lectures before native audiences invited the usual taunts that women on the public rostrum faced, but she comforted herself with the thought that soon ". . . no forcible resistance would be opposed to our public activities." Then presumably enlightenment would flow.[95]

She lectured on literature and on female emancipation, but her fundamental commitment was to the radical political and economic reorganization of American society. Her European-honed beliefs led Madame Anneke to deride reforms and compromises in favor of principled and full transformation. Both she and her husband scorned Germans who made their careers in the mainstream of American politics. They were particularly resentful of Carl Schurz, who had served under Anneke during the military campaigns of 1848-1849. For the Annekes, such politicians were opportunistic self-seekers, but beyond that, their reformist orientation was misguided. The Annekes believed that the regeneration and emancipation of all people, regardless of race or sex, depended upon the replacement of capitalism by communism. Even in Madame Anneke's last years, when she had grown weary and cynical, the communist system remained her ideal. She never developed a scheme for its implementation nor did she even define communism, but she was convinced that both equality and opportunity lay along that path.[96]

Her role within the woman's rights movement involved her in its leadership, sharing highest responsibilities with Susan B. Anthony, Elizabeth Cady Stanton, and others. However, she stood out in that her informal suggestions and formal resolutions tended to be straightforward, unadorned, and uncompromising. She sought not only female suffrage and legal equality, but she attacked religion, nativism, and the temperance movement, all of which many of her colleagues supported; she rejoiced when she saw in the movement ". . . flight [from] religious thinking among women," a sign, she thought, of a greater level of enlightenment.[97]

In the Milwaukee Toechter-Institut, Madame Anneke offered the students a full liberal education. The curriculum included languages, classics, rhetoric, and the arts. The school was ungraded and utilized principles borrowed from a friend who taught at a Froebel kindergarten in Boston. Madame Anneke was determined to prepare her girls adequately for assumption of their full roles in society or, if such participation were to be denied to them, to ready them for a struggle. As a result of her efforts, the school came to command an impressive reputation in the German-speaking community in the Middle West.[98]

Like her predecessors Frances Wright and Ernestine Rose, Madame Anneke was an independent spirit. All of these immigrant feminists had demonstrated in adolescence initiative and commitment, and throughout their lives they proved to be determined individualists. They all rejected relationships which inhibited their independence, and such autonomy was evidently a prerequisite to a sustained marital partnership. All three women married men who endorsed their ideas and whose egos allowed them to encourage their wives' careers (or, in the case of Frances Wright's husband, appeared to do so) and to treat them as equals. These reform-minded husbands, immigrants too, played supportive and subordinate roles in their wives' careers. Each of the women followed pursuits in the United States through which they continued their European-stimulated rebellions against stulifying conditions. All three were shaped in the Old World and, in each case, promoted religious, social, and political goals in the New World which tended to be so sweeping and so critical that they appeared to be prophetic voices out of tune with middle-class and nonradical colleagues in reform movements.[99]

CHAPTER III

Forty-eighter Radicals

THE CONVULSIONS THAT SHOOK THE GERMAN-SPEAKING AREAS OF
Europe in 1848 resulted in a steady stream of German revolutionaries to the United States. Some arrived as early as the closing
months of 1848, and others, after first residing in Switzerland
or England, emigrated to the United States in the early fifties.
They came with their Old World perceptions and began to
apply them to New World conditions. They came as frustrated
revolutionaries, some even as alienated individuals who no
longer were certain that any path other than direct action could
bring about social change. Some had been professional revolutionists, having no other career than that of preparing the way
for social upheaval. No legitimate channels of reform had
existed, and they had sought unsuccessfully to agitate, educate,
and lead would-be followers toward a forceful and systematic
reconstruction of their society. Whether such revolutionaries
would continue to believe that force was necessary and hence
would resort to erecting barricades across the streets of American
cities, or whether their strategies would be modified by the
realization that their best hope lay in the possibility of achieving
change through legal channels, remained to be seen.[1]

These immigrants settled in a country which was then under-
going territorial expansion, sectional strife, industrial growth,
social reformism and, finally, political fragmentation. In the
forties, the United States was expanding. With the absorption
of Mexican lands in the southwest, the entry into the Union of
Texas and California, and the annexation of Oregon territory,
the American Republic attained unchallenged control of all
land from the Atlantic to the Pacific between Mexico and the

[63]

British colonies to the north. As an integral accompaniment to the achievement of such territorial hegemony, however, the Republic found itself clearly dividing into competitive sections. Before mid-century, it had become impossible to grant statehood to a territory without excruciating compromises between the North and the South because of the slavery issue. Simultaneously, the political parties found themselves paying a price for the friction: the Democratic Party shrank to sectional status while the Whigs disintegrated.

In the midst of such strife, the economic and industrial growth of the country continued. The nation's midsection witnessed its first sprawling cities, rising land values, and railway lines, and memories of frontier conditions were displaced by the reality of urban and industrial life. Merchant-capitalists of the pre-industrial economy were overshadowed by factory owners and their machines. These emergent captains of industry and the large labor force upon which they depended struggled against one another over the ten-hour day, wages, and unionization.

By the middle of the century, the multiplying complexities of the maturing society had inspired numerous reform movements. Reformers focused upon educational, criminal, and mental institutions, temperance and female suffrage, pacifism, and most especially and increasingly, upon slavery. The anomaly of the existence of the institution of slavery within a country based upon dedication to freedom and liberty crystallized into the major crisis of nineteenth-century America.

The erstwhile European radicals who viewed the dynamic Republic were struck by both its promises and shortcomings. Having clarity of vision but distorted perspectives, these newcomers incisively analyzed inconsistencies in national performance while often proposing potential solutions and reforms wholly at variance with American trends and mood.

What perhaps most disappointed and troubled the radicals about the United States was the nature of the existing German communities. The Forty-eighters encountered among the masses of Germans in the United States an indifference to political and

social issues. Early in the nineteenth century, most German
immigrants were farmers and artisans who had settled in groups
in Maryland, along the northern shore of the Ohio River, and
finally in the Great Lakes region.[2] Their educational standards
were unusually high for an immigrant group and many believed
their cultural background to be superior to that of native
Americans. They felt bewildered by Puritanism, and opposed
the temperance and Sabbatarian movements. Most were antislavery rather than abolitionist, but many were willing to accept
the institution as an American peculiarity. They respected and
even idealized the shibboleths of equality and democracy and,
consequently, in their political attitudes, they lined up with the
Democrats. To many of the German immigrants in the first half
of the nineteenth century, the Democratic party was symbolized
by Jefferson and Jackson, while the Whig party stood for aristocracy and nativism. But in general the aloofness of the
Germans from American politics as well as their pattern of
scattered residential enclaves mitigated against their developing
political weight in accord with their numbers.[3]

From 1830 until the early 1850's, conscious efforts were made
to create viable, separatist German communities, the most ambitious of which envisioned a German state within the American
Union. Those committed to the idea of a New Germany, preserv-
ing traditional cultural attributes within a republican framework,
sought to utilize the natural inclination of the masses of German
immigrants to settle together. Some even saw their role as
protecting the economic and political interests of the Fatherland
in the United States, but many Germans opposed distinct geo-
graphical or political identity. In any case, after 1830 it was
too late in American history to start a separatist settlement on
a large scale. Only the Mormons met with success, and they,
unlike German colonizers, settled, ultimately, in an undeveloped
and remote area.[4]

Political refugees from Germany first arrived in the United
States after the abortive revolutions of 1830, and it was this
group of exiles which assumed leadership of the Germans in

America. Some of these refugees settled on the land and were
called "Latin Farmers" due to their level of education. Others
became journalists and were responsible for the appearance of
a quality German press in the United States. Their limited political aspirations tended to be in reality cultural. As an example,
at an 1837 convention of German leaders significant interest was
shown in cheaper land for actual settlers and in undermining
nativism. However, the attention of most centered upon preserv-
ing the German language, press, and educational system.[5]

The Forty-eighters were apt to be contemptuous of the political
refugees of the 1830's, known as the *Dreissiger*. They denigrated
their predecessors as liberals rather than radicals, freethinkers
who nonetheless tolerated organized religion, and in general as
failures who had not elevated the lives of the German masses
in the United States. The *Achtundvierziger*, as the Forty-
eighters were known, were prepared to assume leadership of
the Germans in America.

Many of these exiles were cosmopolitans who could more
easily feel at home in urban centers of America than could the
typical immigrant. Few of these refugees experienced language
problems except for the lawyers who were at once handicapped
in the pursuit of their profession. Only a few Forty-eighter
refugees were craftsmen. The most common profession among
them was journalism. A small number of them, awaiting the
anticipated renewal of the revolution, endlessly disputed among
themselves and organized innumerable revolutionary committees. They alienated both native Americans and other German
immigrants by their penchant for criticism. They attacked
American political institutions and cultural mores, alarming the
Germans and inviting nativist counterattacks, and their agnosticism and rationalism irritated everyone else. By the mid-fifties
when they came to accept their residence as permanent, their
proposals for the reconstruction of American institutions had
created both apprehension in and hostility against the German
community.[6]

The Germans were not the only group which produced Forty-eighter refugees. Other nationalities had their political exiles, some of whom settled in the United States. But while some of the Poles, Italians, Hungarians, and other revolutionaries carved out careers for themselves in the United States, the Germans dominated the revolutionary wave of immigrants. Their programs and activities won the greatest attention from their contemporaries and therefore merit the greatest coverage in retrospect.

Doctrinaire Radicals

The most discontented and most determined of the Forty-eighter political refugees were those who arrived with their own visions of the good society and with preconceived notions as to the means of achieving social reconstruction. The more perfected and developed the plan, the less flexibly was the individual able to relate to the United States and to rearrange his program in accord with actuality.

Karl Heinzen (1809-1880) has been called by his biographer an uncompromising and militant radical republican, and yet in the hagiography of the radical immigrants he must be seen as less than extreme. He found American institutions to be imperfect and his thirty-year career as an American journalist was dedicated to a reconstruction within the most fundamental lines of the system. He sought to democratize representation and to make free enterprise and private property less inequitable. His methods were political, constitutional, and propagandistic.[7]

As with so many radical journalists, Heinzen lived a precarious existence in the United States, struggling to keep alive one newspaper after another. Heinzen was more fortunate than the others in terms of the longevity of his papers. He had built a reputation as an outspoken critic of authoritarianism among Germans in America even before he settled in the United States. Once here, he endured a few difficult years, and in 1854 he established his own newspaper, the *Pionier*. Publishing originally in Louisville, then Cincinnati, and New York, he moved the paper to Boston in 1859 and for the remaining twenty years of his life, the *Pionier* was the most successful of the radical German newspapers.[8]

Karl Heinzen was born near Düsseldorf into a middle-class Catholic family and, at the age of twenty-two he followed the family tradition and entered the Prussian bureaucracy. Gradually young Heinzen became critical of government procedures and operations, and in 1840 he resigned. In the next few years Heinzen developed an extensive social and political critique of Prussian society, and in 1844 he had to escape the country in order to avoid criminal prosecution for his writings.[9]

Heinzen and his family lived among other German political refugees in Belgium, Switzerland, and London, exchanging ideas and arguments with Karl Marx, Ferdinand Freiligrath, the Prussian poet, and others. He came to the United States in the winter of 1847-1848 and assumed the editorship of a German-language newspaper published in New York. In March of 1848, after the eruption of the European-wide revolutions, he returned to Germany and participated in the upheaval in Baden. With the defeat of the revolutionaries, he returned to the United States as a permanent resident in 1850.[10]

Heinzen's strength as well as his weakness as a journalist was his incisive pen. His biting sarcasm alienated potential supporters and allies, but he nevertheless clung to his fundamental principle: "think not of compromise, only victory." While in Europe, his fervent intransigence as a republican had led him to the belief that violence might be the only road to successful revolution. Once in the United States, he reassessed his acceptance of violence and tyrannicide, but he adhered to his subsequent strategies with the same uncompromising militancy.[11]

Heinzen's thought was based on rationalism. He had faith in the potential of the individual and abhorred any institution which might dictate to or shackle human devlopment. He wished to free the human mind from imposed theology and systematic philosophies. As an atheist and a rationalist, he considered the basic enemies of man to be organized religion, authoritarian government, and communist doctrine. All three he held to be forces in opposition to man's natural freedom; they symbolized faith and authority, in Heinzen's eyes, rather than reason and liberty.

Heinzen envisioned a society of rational forces in harmony with each other and based on man's innate intelligence. In his republican and atheistic order, each person would be assured of an opportunity for freedom, property, and education. Heinzen did not establish a systematic school of thought, as did other self-styled prophets of his era. His somewhat amorphous vision stemmed from a fundamental optimism and faith in inevitable human and social progress. In that view, he was a child of the Enlightenment, whose ideas were reminiscent of the English-born radicals who had come to the United States a generation earlier.[12]

Heinzen approved of many of the theories upon which the American political and constitutional system was based, but his comprehensive commitment to republican government and equal opportunity led him to see them as imperfectly executed. Heinzen charged that the people did not rule the American Republic but that their representatives were in fact sovereign. The minority lacked equal rights and protection in the face of an overbearing majority. The entire American system, he wrote, had resulted from a series of compromises which negated the ideals of the Republic. State sovereignty served to undercut unity and invited particularism instead of government for and by the whole people. The office of the President suggested to Heinzen an elective king with independent powers. If the people were to rule, Heinzen said, the executive could not claim independence from a legislature which, in turn, could not be unresponsive to the citizenry.[13]

In the first few years of Heinzen's residence in the United States, he developed a program to alleviate the constitutional discrepancies which had become obvious to him. Interestingly, as late as 1853 he published a pamphlet in defense of murder and assassination as legitimate political tactics, but the next year

Heinzen was the moving force behind one of the most famous radical reconstruction platforms presented to the country by recent immigrants.[14]

Heinzen and other German radicals who faulted existing American institutions drew up the detailed Louisville Platform of 1854 which, while inviting the formation of a German reform party, denounced privilege, attacked slavery, and condemned clericalism. The platform advocated the abolition of the Senate and the Presidency. The legislative branch would be unicameral and directly elected while an administrative council would replace the Chief Executive. The Louisville Platform, in addition, endorsed free land for settlers, political rights for blacks and women, and various other economic and social reforms.

To this program, endorsed by several German newspapers throughout the county, Heinzen clung for the rest of his life. But the immediate significance of the platform was the implicit acknowledgment by numbers of German radicals that their stay in the United States was undoubtedly to be permanent. This marked a drastic shift from the Wheeling Congress of 1852, where some Forty-eighters had sketched a full-blown program of world revolution and republicanism. Also of significance, the Louisville Platform inspired attacks by Know-Nothings upon Germans as wild-eyed radicals.[15]

Heinzen was forthright in his criticism of slavery. Unlike other native and immigrant reformers and radicals who shied away from the militant, Heinzen applauded the most zealous of the abolitionists. Heinzen supported Wendell Phillips and William Lloyd Garrison, and consistently demanded political and social equality for the black man. He decried any negotiations over slavery, condemning the Compromise of 1850. A few years later, he hailed John Brown's attack on Harper's Ferry and he supported the Free Soil party and, thereafter, the Republican party. On the eve of the Civil War, he broke with the Republican party (with which he had never fully aligned) and agitated for the organization of a new party committed to equality. Throughout the struggle over slavery, Heinzen maintained a militant posture, and when the issue was apparently buried during Reconstruction, he sadly predicted peonage for the landless, uneducated black Americans.[16]

Heinzen's absolute demand for black equality was paralleled by his stand in favor of full equality for women. Within the German community, militant support of female equality was an even more controversial issue than abolitionism. Most German immigrants thought the female emancipation movement an anomaly and, with the exception of Heinzen, even the German radicals eschewed this issue. In his personal life, Heinzen seemed to thrive on friendships with intelligent women; he knew the various women radicals, such as Ernestine Rose and Mathilde Anneke, joined them in convention, and even published tracts on women's rights under female noms de plume.

He maintained that the issue of female emancipation was the acid test of American democracy. Since the United States had resolved many issues of human rights, this country offered a promising environment for the achievement of the legal, political, religious, and economic emancipation of women. He wrote that women and revolution were natural partners, in that oppressed people recognize the logic of revolutionary movements. Rule by force, money, and priests was gradually pressuring American women to join various reform movements. Women must be granted economic independence, the right to develop all their faculties, liberty to contract marriage and divorce, freedom to engage in premarital sexual relations, and full legal rights and responsibilities.[17]

Karl Heinzen lined up with the various reform movements of mid-century America. He believed that the state and society must allow to each individual full opportunities for complete development. Therefore, he supported prison reform, the public school movement, the eight-hour day, the cooperative movement, public works projects for the unemployed, and graduated income and inheritance taxes. Through his newspaper he vigorously carried on the struggle for American reform movements within the German community.[18]

He favored the free enterprise system and the institution of private property. "Capital itself is not evil," he wrote, but merely in need of reform. Heinzen, uneasy with economic theory, rejected the idea of determinism and simply stressed the importance of economic opportunity as the basis of political democracy. Heinzen would give all men the chance to work and to acquire property. Such opportunity was inherent in Heinzen's just society.[19]

Heinzen always regretted his inability to reach the American public due to his inadequate English. It did not occur to him, as his biographer, Carl Wittke, has written, that his social and political programs often were so extraneous to American traditions that he could not have attracted much native support. But, it should also be noted that his own odyssey as a radical critic demonstrated surprising adaptability and a marked influence within the German community in America. As a transplanted radical, he was able to reshape his own thinking in response to the American environment and to develop programs in terms of reform rather than revolution. As the editor of the longest-lived radical foreign-language newspaper of his era, his voice was heard and his ideas discussed, and thus he played an important role in involving the educated German public in American issues.[20]

Wilhelm Weitling (1808-1871), a journeyman tailor, was another of the Forty-eighter immigrant radicals. Ideologically, Weitling filled a gap between the "gut radicalism" of Heinzen and the philosophical revolutionary theories of the Marxist immigrants. Somewhat unique among the theorists because of his impoverished working-class background, Weitling served as a transitional figure, a link between utopian and scientific communism. Interestingly, as a member of the working class, he minimized class conflict and, although an agnostic, he nevertheless emphasized religion and morality.

Weitling was born in Magdeburg during the French occupation, the illegitimate child of a servant woman and a French soldier. The ill-educated Weitling spent his early manhood as a tailor until he was exposed to working-class revolutionary groups and secret societies in Paris in the late 1830's. He absorbed the programs of Fourier and Cabet, while retaining a working man's contempt for theory. Weitling won prominence in the political underground of France, Switzerland, and Belgium as an organizer, agitator, orator, and writer. As late as the early 1840's he was probably the most influential radical among German workers abroad.[21]

Weitling was an incorrigible optimist. He always imagined a project successfully completed almost before it was begun. He mistook the thought for the deed, as Robert Owen before him, and throughout his life he never failed to overestimate the possibilities of success. Weitling seemed incapable of a realistic assessment of society and of human nature. In that weakness lay the particular poignancy of his career.

His major writings were completed in Europe by 1843 and thereafter his basic ideas changed very little. He emigrated to the United States in the winter of 1846-1847, briefly returned to Central Europe at the outbreak of the revolution, and settled in New York in 1849. There he edited a German-language newspaper, organized German-speaking workers, and served as the administrator of an ill-fated experimental colony in Iowa. In the mid-fifties Weitling withdrew from activism and supported his family through tailoring.[22]

Weitling and Marx participated in the same revolutionary circle in Brussels. Their basic approaches to communism conflicted, however, and their final break in 1846 occurred over a tactical issue: Marx condemned Hermann Kriege, a radical publisher in New York, for Kreige's alliance with American reform forces, while Weitling insisted that American conditions supported such a strategy. The economic determinism of Karl Marx was unintelligible to Weitling who rejected the Marxian view of man as more object than actor. He also repudiated the idea of self-interest as man's only motivation. Weitling stressed individual moral responsibility rather than the class struggle. As he saw it, communism must be based on social ethics.

From his unsystematic reading of French and English utopian socialists in combination with his keen awareness of the debasement of the western worker, Weitling became committed to the goal of guaranteed political, economic, and social equality His system of thought was predicated on the necessity of a harmony or balance between an individual's capacities and needs. Communism, with its planned economy and community property, was the only social organization which could insure an equitable balance in production, exchange, and consumption. The new order was to be achieved not by forces inevitably destroying the present system but, rather, through enlightened, almost messianic leadership. His confidence in his own ability to lead the masses to a successful revolution as well as his belief that popular sovereignty was a mirage, allowed him to endorse the idea of a temporary dictatorship in order to establish communism.[23]

Weitling was an impatient critic of the United States. Every problem seemed to him to be rooted in the existence of private property. He attributed the evil of slavery to private land ownership and indicted the legislative system as representative of the propertied only. He denounced American politics as ridiculous and he wasted little time supporting reform movements, despite his earlier approval of alliances with reformers. He believed that the only solution for inequities was full-scale revolution. The one contemporary conflict in which he involved himself was the labor struggle.[24]

Weitling assumed as his immediate task the centralization of German labor. In general, the labor movement in the United States was amorphous in the early fifties, lacking a firm direction. Unrest was prevalent while goals were uncertain. American workers did not clearly see themselves as a class and they still supported variegated reform movements. German immigrant workers played a distinct role in the antebellum labor movement, for they tended to exude an intuitive class consciousness that native workers lacked. Some of their social clubs and mutual aid societies evolved into class-conscious unions which Weitling tried to dominate and shape in accord with his own ideas.[25]

He supported ongoing strike activity while attempting to convince the workers that sporadic efforts were hopeless. He proposed to expand the existing German Central Committee of the United Trades of New York into a national organization, and in October, 1850, he brought about the meeting of the first national Labor Congress ever held in the United States. Delegates representative of four thousand workers throughout the country attended and approved Weitling's pet scheme of banks of exchange and cooperative associations. Local organizations were to deposit their funds with a central bank of exchange in return for paper money, meanwhile storing their raw and finished products as security. Wages would be paid in script in accord with the amount of labor expended. The Congress formed a Workingmen's League and resolved that upon the fruits of cooperation would be founded colonies of workers' republics.[26]

Membership boomed during the next few months, but when the League failed to find jobs for the unemployed, never its purpose, it quickly declined. Despite Weitling's optimism, not one bank of exchange was ever founded and a second Congress was never held. Weitling's modification of the exchange system, central to his hope of abolishing monopoly, if not capitalism itself, was too abstract and distant a goal for the workers. Strikes and demonstrations were tactics easily understood, and some interest existed in cooperatives, a notion imported by earlier immigrant radicals, whereas Weitling's program appeared unrealistic to them. Its brief success was directly due to his notoriety but Weitling's influence lasted only a year. Concomitant with his demise as a labor leader was the fact that the outlook of the German workers themselves was changing. Increased contact with English-speaking workers led them to absorb the indigenous notions of individualism and opportunity within the system, and as a result the influence of leaders such as Weitling faded.[27]

The epilogue to Weitling's activist career was his attempt

to breathe life into his communist theories in a colony near Dubuque, Iowa. In October of 1851 Weitling visited Communia, an agricultural collective recently established by two dozen Swiss immigrants. Weitling had known some of the colonists associated with Communia and admired their experiment, and when he finally arrived there he was euphoric. "Now I stand for the first time in my life on the holy ground of a brotherly community," he wrote, and immediately determined that the struggling community must embody his program. The Workingmen's League and the as yet unorganized banks of exchange would be consolidated at Communia, and the full development of the communist experiment would culminate in a network of colonies.[28]

With the framework of his system apparently in existence at Communia, Weitling sought only to perfect it. He invested the funds of the Workingmen's League in return for the assets of the colony. Weitling soon consolidated the two enterprises and he himself gained legal possession of the deed of trust.[29]

At once, the colony's meager resources began to devour the League's assets and he was forced to revise the colony's constitution, ironically permitting capitalist inroads in an effort to achieve self-sufficiency. In a desperate effort to salvage the situation, Weitling became colony administrator in November, 1853. Tension and hostility grew and Weitling's correspondence reveals his own agonizing over his lack of authority and eventually the emergence of a martyr complex. Communia collapsed into bankruptcy in 1855 and with it the assets of the Workingmen's League and Weitling's newspaper.[30]

Weitling was an immigrant radical who understood the American environment sufficiently to eschew secret societies and violence. He organized workers against the system of monetary exchange, and played an early role in the effort to centralize the labor movement. The abrupt decline in his influence and his subsequent retirement were not so much reflective of misreading conditions as of psychological self-deception. Weitling's person-

ality and outlook lent themselves to illusions and he was likely
to misjudge possibilities anywhere.

Karl Marx never came to the United Sates but Marxism arrived
in New York at the early date of 1851 through the immigration
of one of Marx's disciples, Joseph Weydemeyer. Weydemeyer
(1818-1866) was a young Westphalian who served for six years
as a Prussian artillery officer. During this period he and a number of other young officers, including later revolutionaries such
as Fritz Anneke, August Willich, and Friedrich von Beust,
came under the influence of the Cologne *Rheinische Zeitung*
edited by Marx. By 1845 Weydemeyer had abandoned his military career and became a student and propagandist of Marxism.[31]

As a journalist in Brussels and Westphalia, Weydemeyer
attempted to lead disgruntled workers away from their secret
societies. He wished to imbue them with the Marxist point of
view that material considerations were the basis of social change.
Weydemeyer was an organizer for the Communist League and
hoped to establish labor parties with worker support. During the
Revolution of 1848 he was active as a journalist and he opposed
the Frankfort convention in favor of popula⸗ initiatives. After
the demise of the revolution, Weydemeyer fled into exile, where
he was unable to support his family. Defeated by the censorship
prevalent almost everywhere in Europe, he reluctantly decided
on immigration to the United States. Both Marx and Engels
consoled him that useful organizational tasks among the Germans there awaited a revolutionary so well grounded in theory.[32]

Friederich Sorge (see below) credited Weydemeyer with introducing to the American labor movement the recognition that
social conflicts are economically-based class struggles. Weydemeyer hoped to liberate the workers from bourgeois labor
leaders and nonscientific communists. Simultaneously, he sought
to involve them in political action joined to union activity.
He wanted to unite the workers by undercutting the divisiveness
of the nationality barriers which fragmented the American movement. He addressed himself to immediate issues, such as the

ten-hour day and the abolition of child labor, while at the same time stressing the long-range need of educating the workers for the inevitable revolution. Weydemeyer advised against Luddite destruction of machinery and wrote that the growth of industry and the accumulation of capital were unavoidable and even symbolic of social progress. The workers must simply prepare for their own role of rendering that expansion socially responsible.[33]

Weydemeyer prophesied that the transition to the classless order would be violent. He envisioned the working class "tearing down the barriers which keep it from enjoying the riches of this earth . . ." at the very moment when the cycle of business crisis demonstrated capitalism to be fatally weakened. Thereafter, the concentration of capital and the instruments of production would be controlled by the state under "the dictatorship of the proletariat," wrote Weydemeyer, in the first article ever written on this subject. It has been suggested that he emphasized implicitly the seizure of power itself and the role of the leadership while Marx stressed the primacy of the masses. If so, such a position would be indicative of Weydemeyer's familiarity with pre-Marxist theories of personal dictatorships held by such revolutionaries as the Parisian Louis Auguste Blanqui and Weydemeyer's German-American rival Wilhelm Weitling. Nonetheless, the promotion of this key Marxist idea began on the western shores of the Atlantic.[34]

Weydemeyer's American career did not focus upon efforts to seize power but, rather, on the education of the workers. Upon arrival, he immediately settled into his tasks for, unlike many Forty-eighters, Weydemeyer recognized that a successful revolution in Germany was not imminent and therefore his revolutionary arena was destined to be the United States. His first impressions left him far from sanguine for, as he wrote to Marx, "I don't think there is another place where one encounters the shopkeeper's mentality in more revolting nakedness."

He began to publish what were invariably short-lived propaganda newspapers and he organized two successive leagues of

German workers, the earliest Marxist organizations in the United States. The first, the Proletarian League of New York, was virtually stillborn in 1852. The second, the German Workers League, later called the American Workers League, was organized in 1853, ostensibly to satisfy worker interest in a central trades council. The League demanded better conditions and hours, decent wages and welfare reforms, and, seeking to relate Marxism to American possibilities, free higher education and frontier lands guaranteed to associations of farmers. Weydemeyer succeeded in organizing the membership into political clubs representative of more than half the wards of New York City and devoid of nationality or occupational divisions. The League's political program included the nationalization of major resources. Its basic argument was that new economic conditions required American institutions to be revised from their eighteenth-century foundations. Weydemeyer appeared to be thriving.[35]

In reality, however, the League was not developing within the framework which Weydemeyer had imposed upon it. It received greater support and contributions from abroad than it did in New York.[36] Weydemeyer recognized that the League was fundamentally a German workers group, differing little from a mutual aid society. He gradually withdrew from his activities, and he moved from New York to the Midwest in 1856 where he lectured and propagandized, while supporting his family as a surveyor and notary. He, like many other Forty-eighters, promoted the Republican party on the eve of the Civil War. In Weydemeyer's case, his role was consistent with his belief in supporting progressive movements rather than remaining aloof from existing political issues. He fought in the Civil War, with some of the same men he had served beside in the Prussian army. After the war, he accepted a minor public office, possibly indicative of uncertainty of direction, but he soon died in the cholera epidemic of 1866.[37]

The significance of Weydemeyer's American career lay in his effort to solve two serious problems hampering the development of the American labor movement: its ethnic and craft divisions and its tentative and ambivalent approach to political participation. But Weydemeyer, perhaps premature in his efforts, never reached more than a handful of workers and whether many of them accepted his theoretical predilections was never clear.

Weydemeyer, like Heinzen and Weitling, had utilized political and constitutional channels in order to perfect the American Republic. None of these radicals operated outside the legal system nor ever found themselves restricted in their pursuits. Neither a militant like Heinzen, seeking to build political reform movements based on his own frame of reference, nor even a professional revolutionist like Weydemeyer, a disciple of Marx, promoting economic and social transformation, believed that conspiracies or force was necessary. Because of the existence of civil rights and liberties in the United States, especially the freedom of the press, radical Forty-eighters recognized that the American environment presented them with the opportunity to persuade others to their points of view. These doctrinaires thus responded to American conditions. Their alienation from their own societies had not been so pervasive as to prevent their recognition of the possibilities of gradual progress within a constitutional system.

As figures representative of the various revolutionary Forty-eighters in the United States, Heinzen, Weitling, and Weydemeyer found their new home a viable arena in which to pursue, if not to fulfill, their own ends.

Militant Abolitionists

Many German immigrants ignored the slavery issue and the increasing controversy over abolitionism. The German immigrant might admit a basic hostility to slavery but in fact he was indifferent to the institution: he had his own problems and interests. While he most likely did not own slaves because he did not live in the South, he preferred that slavery remain territorially limited in order that more areas of the country not be closed to free labor.

The German immigrant's position on slavery varied in accord with his residence. A German in the North would be far more likely to articulate his discomfort with the system, while a Southern-based immigrant would hold his tongue, and perhaps gradually adopt the Southern point of view. Above all, there was the insecurity of the newcomer that encouraged an uncritical posture toward indigenous institutions. Only when personally threatened by slavery would German immigrants openly sympathize with the abolitionist movement. As an example, in Baltimore, the only large city south of the Mason-Dixon line with a sizable German population, German ˋartisans supported anti-slavery forces in hopes of eliminating slave labor competition.[38]

Leaders of the German-American community prior to the arrival of the Forty-eighters tended to support the Democratic party, as cited above. Even when the party began to represent only the South, they clung to their traditional alliance, at least until the Kansas-Nebraska Act of 1854. But the Forty-eighters at once joined the battle against slavery. Some opposed the institution for moral and ethical reasons, others on humanitarian grounds, and some opposed slavery because it seemed inherent in the general struggle against privilege. These critics, unlike the *Dreissiger*, lacked a stake in the Democratic party. Therefore, they were free to voice their opposition to this American anomaly.

A number of Forty-eighters did not hesitate to condemn slavery within the confines of the Southern states. Heinzen's forthright abolitionism and his demand for full equality for blacks was not tempered by his residence in Kentucky (see the Louisville Platform above). The destruction of the press of the paper for which he then worked, the *Herold des Westens*, possibly a case of arson, was followed by Know-Nothing riots against the Germans of Louisville. Heinzen's countrymen were glad to see him depart from Louisville and after 1855 they concentrated upon rebuilding their community reputation as solid, conservative citizens.[40]

Carl Heinrich Schnauffer (1823-1854) published the only explicitly antislavery newspaper, German or English, in Maryland. The *Wecker*, founded in 1851 as a mouthpiece for the Forty-eighters of Baltimore, was a militant sheet, based on the publisher's own humanitarian inclinations. He settled in the South for personal reasons rather than as an abolitionist, but once there Schnauffer stood uncompromisingly for emancipation. He dared mob attack which, indeed, finally erupted after his death and endangered his surviving family.[41]

Schnauffer was one of the most talented of the literary figures among the immigrants and, while not fundamentally a radical, he supported some of the programs offered by revolutionaries seeking to found a German political party in the United States. Schnauffer had been an aspiring young poet from Stuttgart who came under the influence of Friedrich Hecker and Gustav Struve. He was drawn into political activity by these two radical democrats, and his student career at Heidelberg ended with his joining his mentors in the Baden Revolution. After two escapes to Switzerland, he finally came to the United States from England in 1851.

Exile was a blow to Schnauffer and his early days in this country were spent mourning his lost Germany. But his need to earn a living and his absolute commitments to liberty and individual dignity led him to assume the role of crusading editor in American causes. From his Southern base, he wrote of freedom, human welfare, and democracy. His historical significance rests with his title of "Tyrtaeus of the Baden Revolution." The Turner movement in the United States, a fraternal German association, considered him one of the most gifted poets. His constant literary theme was the worldwide revolution of liberation. In the history of the Upper South his name stands as one of the very few in the fifties who opposed slavery and nativism

and supported education, enlightenment, and freedom at a time
and place when silence offered an easier path.[42]

Several German communities existed in southwestern Texas in
the 1850's as a result of unsuccessful efforts to found a New Germany there prior to the entrance of Texas into the Union, and
a German flavor dominated portions of the area until after the
Civil War.[43] The Germans of Texas began to organize in 1853-
1854 as a means of protecting themselves against rising nativist
currents. They sought to win political power in the Southwest
commensurate with their numbers. A local German journalist
was responsible for endowing the movement with an abolitionist
aura which turned both Americans and Germans against him
and eventually forced him to migrate to the North. Dr. Carl
Daniel Adolf Douai (1819-1888) was a teacher whose participation in the German revolution had caused him to emigrate
to the United States in 1852. After settling in San Antonio, Douai
had shifted from teaching to editing and publishing.

The Texas Germans adopted the organizational pattern of
Germans in various other states who were becoming aligned
loosely as state branches of the self-protective, short-lived league
Bund Freier Maenner. In convention the Texas Germans adopted
a platform which was antinativist, reformist, and antislavery.
While the *Bund's* platform explicitly had condemned slavery,
those meeting in San Antonio rationalized that slavery, acknowledged as an institution incompatible with democratic
government, nevertheless was protected by states' rights.[44]

Following the convention in May, 1854, an imbroglio erupted.
The slavery plank of the platform, publicized by Adolf Douai
in his *San Antonio Zeitung,* split the German community and
inspired attacks by proslavery Texas newspapers. The Germans,
organizing only for self-protection, felt themselves threatened as
they had not been earlier.[45]

Adolf Douai, from the moment of his arrival in southwestern
Texas, had nurtured hopes of a grand alliance against slavery
that would result in a separate, free-soil state of West Texas.
He sought to unite Northerners, who might be encouraged to

settle in the area if a railroad were built, Mexicans, who were antislavery, and Germans, who he felt would become overt free-soilers if they recognized potential allies. Douai calculated through rough population figures that southwestern Texas was forty percent German and Mexican and soon would be fifty percent non-Yankee. Thus, the possibility of a strong free-soil party which could prevent the expansion of slavery into the area seemed a viable idea.[46]

Douai believed that the foreign born could save not only Texas but the country as a whole from its bondage to the peculiar institution. It appeared to him that the non-slaveholding portion of the country was in fact helpless before the slaveholders. He wrote that 150,000 despots controlled the American Republic, that non-slaveholders had to be educated to the fact of their own economic subjugation and, that "the beginning must be made by us foreigners."[47]

Douai tried to reach out to the Americans in the area by publishing sections of his paper in English and by including contributions from American friends, such as Frederick Law Olmsted, then preparing his series on slavery for *The New York Times*. Douai had met Olmsted and his brother, John, during their tour of Texas in 1853. He was able to provide the Olmsteds with data to support Frederick Olmsted's observations on Texas as a slave state, and the latter in return helped Douai to secure loans in the East for his newspaper. Olmsted was also able to guide and reinforce some of Douai's judgments about the possibility of persuading Americans to his point of view.[48]

The publicity surrounding the convention and Douai's propaganda for a free-soil party marked the beginning of the end of the potential antislavery movement in the area. Rumors spread that Douai had been hired by Northern abolitionists. His advertisers withdrew their support, and shareholders and subscribers abandoned the paper. Aware of violent incidents elsewhere, Douai feared the destruction of his office, or even lynching. Increased financial assistance from the Olmsteds, who sought to channel money to him from Eastern pacifists desirous of an alternative to contributing arms to Kansas, failed to alleviate Douai's problems. He felt increasingly isolated and finally, in 1856, abandoned the South and moved to New York.[49]

Douai went on to a varied career in the North, involving education, journalism, and politics. He was an active participant in a number of radical enterprises. He collaborated with Karl Heinzen on the *Pionier* for a time, spread Marxist propaganda, and joined a "dump Lincoln" movement during the Civil War over the President's foot-dragging on emancipation. In many instances, his outspoken courage was clear, whether it was informing Americans of what he called their tradition-bound hypocrisy or deriding German nationalism. However, his other adventures pale beside his Texas experience which remains a notable episode in the antislavery movement in the South.[50]

The careers of Schnauffer and Douai as abolitionists in the Southern states involved the most intense and direct Forty-eighter confrontations with slavery. But almost without exception, every politically active Forty-eighter publicly opposed the peculiar institution. Whatever the thrust of the individual's career or his approach to social issues, his antagonism to slavery was clear. The form which that opposition assumed ran the gamut from active abolitionism to sanguine beliefs that the system would be supplanted. While a Karl Heinzen attacked slavery directly from within its heartland, a Wilhelm Weitling assumed that the future egalitarian order would erase all inequities. At the same time, the Forty-eighter politicians of the ilk of Friedrich Kapp, Friedrich Hassaurek, and Carl Schurz, joined the battle within the highest ranks of the Republican party. And while the strategies thus varied widely, so too did the goal. Like the Yankees, these immigrant abolitionists disagreed among themselves over the issue of political and social equality after emancipation.

The Forty-eighters achieved some success in awakening their countrymen to the fact that the real issue in the fifties was not temperance but slavery, which threatened to undermine their adopted nation. Perhaps reluctantly, numbers of Germans came

to emulate the Forty-eighters' support for the antislavery movement. On the other hand, the nativist phenomenon, which most
directly frightened the immigrants, was stimulated by German
support for abolitionism. Thus, potential danger lay in the very
essence of moral victory.

Radical Politicians

Any division suggested between the abolitionist movement and
the political developments of the 1850's is intrinsically arbitrary
and might even seem distorted. Abolitionism and politics were
inherently joined, and for Forty-eighters involved in the struggle
against slavery, a role in American politics was accessible. Those
immigrants whose radicalism lent itself to working within the
system became deeply immersed in the organization and growth
of a new national party. In this role German radicals found
themselves on the center stage of the American panorama.

Their arrival occurred during the climax of the crisis over
slavery and the disintegration of the political parties. The
newcomers' taste of political leadership in the Old World, added
to their interest in building a solid foundation for Germans in
the United States, thrust them into the heart of the struggle.
Moreover, as an American ambassador later remarked to Bismarck, the Forty-eighters were able to discuss the crisis of the
fifties in a distinctive manner; not only did they point out constitutional and moral issues, but they emphasized the manner
in which the nation as a whole was experiencing fragmentation.
The Forty-eighters argued against compromise; slavery must
be confronted by a principled political party because it was
wrong and because without its overthrow the nation could not
stabilize and survive.[51]

The Kansas-Nebraska Act of 1854 coincided with a flurry of
German organizational activity in reaction to Know-Nothingism.
The Forty-eighter leadership of these defensive efforts was
outraged by the Kansas-Nebraska Act and marshaled its forces
against the Democratic party. German newspapers opposed the

bill at a ratio of ten to one and, while the German masses were not so easily persuaded to switch political parties, this event provided the catalyst for German leaders to abandon the Democrats. Even some of the bickering between the Forty-eighters and the earlier leadership was mitigated in an effort to wrest the German vote from the Democrats' grip. However, German leaders lacked an alternative to offer the voters of their community. The Whigs remained identified with nativism, and a separate German party would mean too narrow a base. While a few former Democrats experimented with both of these options, most waited for the emergence of an antislavery, pro-immigrant, progressive political party.[52]

With the appearance of the Republican party late in 1854, a symbiotic relationship between the party and the Forty-eighters rapidly evolved. While the earlier German leaders came over only grudgingly, almost all of the Forty-eighter activists supported the new party and, in return, the Republicans offered financial support to their various newspapers. In the 1856 national election, Forty-eighter radicals avidly campaigned in the German community for the election to the presidency of Republican John C. Frémont. In the Old Northwest especially, Germans appeared on campaign platforms for the Republican party and ran for office themselves in Illinois and Wisconsin. Some won state offices as Republicans in 1856 and 1858, but their efforts to bring their countrymen en masse into the new party was only marginally successful. The German community still viewed the Republican party as a hotbed of nativists, temperance workers, and Sabbatarians.[53]

A crisis occurred in 1859 when the German Republicans found their proselytizing for the party stymied by the passage in Massachusetts of a Republican-supported nativist amendment to the state constitution. This measure, which has been described as striking the German Republicans with an intensity comparable to the effect of John Brown's raid exploding in the South, delayed suffrage for two years following naturalization. Despite the disappointment, however, they clung to the party, convinced that national Republican leaders such as William H. Seward and Abraham Lincoln opposed nativist legislation. Moreover, various party conventions and state committees denounced the Massachusetts amendment. It seemed clear to the German Republicans that they had sufficient strength within the party to crush incipient nativist efforts.[54]

The national convention of 1860 verified such confidence. While the German masses had not streamed into the party (some held back especially by Catholic hostility to Forty-eighter atheism), the Germans at the convention had sufficient influence to apply pressure for the incorporation of the so-called Dutch planks into the Republican platform. Various German Republicans, including Adolf Douai and Joseph Weydemeyer, met and hammered out their own platform on the eve of the convention's opening at the Wigwam in Chicago. They demanded equality for foreign-born citizens, homestead legislation, and the admission of Kansas as a free state. With party acceptance of these measures and the nomination of an acceptable candidate—Abraham Lincoln—the German Republicans embarked on speaking tours to win the German vote for Lincoln.[55]

Legends abound among German-Americans claiming unified German support for Lincoln. However, the Germans who had played dynamic roles in the rise of the Republican party were unable to deliver the vote. While Germans held the balance of power in several midwestern states, various studies conclude that only in Illinois did the German vote put the state in the Republican column. Thus, the Forty-eighters had limited success, but Lincoln rewarded many of them for their efforts with diplomatic and consular appointments.[56]

Among the Republican activists were Friedrich Hecker, Lincoln's running mate in 1856 for elector-at-large in Illinois; journalist Georg Schneider, a close friend of Lincoln's and a founder of the Republican party in the Prairie State; Gustav Körner (one of the Dreissiger), a Democratic lieutenant governor of Illinois in the fifties who switched parties and became a spiritual relative of the Forty-eighters; Reinhold Solger, a professor and author whose Boston residence enabled him to oppose the Two-Year Amendment from its inception; and Gustav Struve, an eccentric New York journalist who was Schnauffer's mentor and a sometime collaborator of Heinzen's. The careers which best highlight the experiences of Forty-eighter politicians in the fifties were those of Friedrich Kapp, Friedrich Hassaurek, and Carl Schurz.

All three were political refugees who arrived in the United States between 1849 and 1852. After a period of adjustment in which each floundered, sorting out impressions and criticisms of the United States, they settled into successful careers. All took law degrees and dabbled in journalism. The three men campaigned vigorously in the German community for the Republican party in each of its antebellum election bids. They all came to hold high government positions in return for their services to the party. Kapp finally returned to Germany while Schurz, alone among the Forty-eighter radical activists, came to be known as an American political leader. These men were able to play prominent roles in mainstream politics because their radicalism did not involve drastic alterations in the American framework as was true of the Marxists but, rather, modifications within the existing system.[57]

Friedrich Kapp (1824-1884) spent five frustrating years between his arrival in the United States in 1850 and his naturalization in 1855. He lived the insecure existence of a free-lance journalist in a strange land. He traveled across the country as far as Texas, where he visited in the San Antonio area, and thereafter wrote and lectured on slavery. He published scholarly biographies of Germans in America, including Von Steuben and De Kalb, and histories of German settlements in the United States. Kapp also served as a correspondent for European newspapers and was an editor of *Atlantische Studien,* a journal published in Göttingen which sought to present a realistic picture of American conditions and hardships to potential German immigrants. In 1855, after his initial disillusionment with American ideals and his despair over disunity in the Fatherland, he settled in New York, opening a law firm in partnership with two other Forty-eighters.[58]

Kapp never really felt comfortable in the United States. Although his law career flourished, he did not cease to look upon himself as a displaced European. He sent his children to Germany for their education, and he himself continually sought ways in which he might some day resume his life there. He always believed that the immature American civilization was far inferior to German culture and he described American priorities as misguided. The nation as a whole cared only for the practical, neglecting the life of the mind. He wrote bitterly to Ludwig Feuerbach, the German philosopher, that it had been a mistake to come to America to win emancipation from European prisons. Here he encountered many freedoms, he acknowledged, but the atmosphere limited intellectual liberty. He supported American ideals but the "fossilized constitution" served as the framework of a country in which traditions had become more tyrannical than political despotism. Constitutionally protected freedoms did not mean freedom of speech or of press.[59]

He stormed against the domination of the country by the wealthy and against the lack of interest of the merchant class in politics. Kapp indicted the spoils system and the corruption of municipal government which he found in New York and other large cities. But at least political failures, as opposed to cultural inadequacies, might be rectified and he hoped that Lincoln's election would result in self-government for all Americans, with the North freed of the South's yoke and the slaves at last emancipated.[60]

Kapp had been a communist in his youth, but had found revolution-making an empty life. In the United States he moved away from systematic philosophies. He became less radical than reformist, militant only in his scorn for religious influences. Aside from his cultural chauvinism, he focused upon those American inequities which he thought could be solved within the existing system. At first he had joined the Whigs with whom he felt culturally comfortable. But his belief in rationalism and his hostility to slavery, an issue he always treated as an episode in the eternal battle between freedom and bondage, led him to the Republican party. As a successful New Yorker whose home was a salon for the educated Germans of the city, he attempted to draw his countrymen to the Republican ticket. In 1856 he campaigned throughout New York State, in 1860 he was a delegate to the national Republican convention, and in 1867 Kapp was appointed New York State Commissioner of Immigration. He held that position for three years when, upon completion of German unification, he rushed back to the Fatherland. There he was elected to the Reichstag and from that base, opposed the authoritarian system of ˋBismarck. At last there was one Germany, making it possible for Kapp to enjoy partial fulfillment of his dreams of forty-eight.[61]

Friedrich Hassaurek (1831-1885) was one of the youngest Forty-eighter refugees to build a political career in the United States and was also one of the most tempestuous. He arrived in New York at the age of eighteen, a twice-wounded Viennese revolutionary, and settled in Cincinnati. The "Queen City" was then a riverboat town of frontier radicalism, urban commercialism, Southern influences, and social fermentation. One-half of its population was foreign born; sixty percent of those were German.[62]

Hassaurek edited the Cincinnati *Hochwächter*, a weekly, and from that editorial rostrum, he addressed the less conservative elements of the German community. At the time he advocated socialist measures and often advised workers on their needs and rights. His newspaper was essentially an anticlerical sheet. Hassaurek's agnosticism led him into controversy as he challenged religious orthodoxy in its many guises. As a founder of the local Free Men's Society, Hassaurek engaged in a series of public debates with Wilhelm Nast, the patriarch of German Methodism. When a representative of the Vatican visited Cincinnati, Hassaurek participated in a demonstration against the Papal Nuncio. Violence erupted and resulted in Hassaurek's arrest for inciting a riot. He often peppered his writings with anti-Catholic statements, but generally he saw little difference among variations of orthodox religions and castigated them all for hypocrisy and ignorance.[63]

Hassaurek's involvement politically was propelled by the rise of Know-Nothingism. His residence in Cincinnati exposed him directly to the nativist thrust, and as an editor and, after 1855, a member of the city's Common Council and a well-known criminal lawyer, he dominated the defensive movement. The local politicians courted the large German vote in the city, and Hassaurek found his support valued as a link to that community. Even Governor Salmon P. Chase consulted Hassaurek on the German response to a possible amendment to the Ohio constitution delaying suffrage for one year after naturalization.[64]

Gradually Hassaurek became engulfed in the free-soil movement and national politics. While initially his reputation had been primarily limited to the German community, he became attracted to American issues and abandoned the campaigns of the early fifties to found a radical German party. As his American involvements deepened, he drifted away from German militants like Heinzen, who later despised Hassaurek as a turncoat. Hassaurek's European-inspired revolutionary ardor in fact had moderated and by 1856 his main ambition was to build a strong Republican party. He became the most active party organizer among Germans in Ohio, and the founder of the Cincinnati branch of the party. He was a skilled and fearless orator in German and English, renowned for responding to hecklers by placing a revolver on the speaker's lectern. Republicans in Indiana and Illinois and other states deluged him with invitations to address their German-speaking citizens.[65]

In 1856 Hassaurek campaigned throughout the state of Ohio for Frémont, although he personally disliked the evolving American custom of nominating generals for the Presidency. He addressed German audiences, arranged for the translation of Frémont's biography into German, and even tried to reach out to former Know-Nothings to bring them into the Republican fold. In 1860, while being mentioned for the Republican nomination for Congress from Hamilton County (Cincinnati), Hassaurek served as a delegate to the national convention, participated in the "Deutsches Haus" conference, and took credit for German Republican votes. Whether or not his campaign contributions were crucial in Cincinnati's vote for Lincoln, as was claimed, Hassaurek was rewarded by Lincoln for his years of service to the party by appointment as minister to Ecuador.[66]

Hassaurek clung to what he considered progressive policies.[67] He remained loyal to Lincoln in 1864, unlike German radicals who abandoned the President as too dilatory on the issue of emancipation. Years later, in 1872, Hassaurek joined the Liberal Republican movement and sought to lead German voters away from Grant, as earlier he had tried to bring them over to Lincoln. His career to the end remained that of a German in American politics whose constituency was the ethnic voter. Hassaurek, like most of his comrades, could not escape his label and win acknowledgment as an American political figure.

Carl Schurz was the one exception. Only a handful of years lay between his immigration in 1852 and his national prominence during the presidential election campaign of 1860. By the start of the Civil War, Schurz was recognized not only as the spokesman of the German community, in the eyes of the American press and public, but also as a leading representative of Republican opinion in the Middle West.

Carl Schurz (1829-1906), as the most renowned and the last of the Forty-eighters to be considered here, enjoyed a career unique among his peers. His years in the United States were marked by immersion in political events. A world apart from some of the professional revolutionists whose lives touched his in 1848, Schurz became a professional politician. His family life was circumscribed by political necessities, his income and finances were never stable, and his schedule was dictated by party considerations. The consummate man of politics, he found his calling in the Republican party in 1854.

Schurz came from modest circumstances. He was born into a

Catholic family which resided near Cologne, and somehow survived, albeit insecurely, on the father's inadequate school-master's income. At the outbreak of the 1848 revolution, Schurz was an eighteen-year-old student in Bonn who looked forward to a career as a professor. He participated in the Baden Revolution, during which he was wounded and imprisoned. After his escape, he rescued from the fortress at Spandau a favorite professor, Gottfried Kinkel, who had been a prominent democratic revolutionary leader. As a result of liberating Kinkel, young Schurz became a celebrity among other emigrés with whom he lived in Switzerland, France, and England. But he became discouraged and impoverished. Schurz reacted boldly to the news of the coup d'état of Louis Napoleon in December, 1851. Europe seemed to him hopeless. He set off with his young wife for the United States where he was determined to follow a career as a lecturer while waiting for the renewal of the revolution.[68]

The first two years of Schurz's American odyssey were un-eventful. Exploiting his wife's dwindling family funds, Schurz devoted all of his time and energies to the study of the English language. Rigorously disciplining himself, he quickly gained facility in English, and thereafter set out to tour the country. He visited Washington and, though he found Congress unim-pressive in comparison with the formality and decorum of European parliaments, he came alive. As he wrote his wife, "When I come in touch with this atmosphere of political activity, I feel the old fire of 1848 coursing in my veins. . . ."[69]

Schurz had found his vocation. He settled in Wisconsin, where a large German population and an unstructured political situation seemed to offer opportunity. His need to bestride the center stage and his willingness to expend all of his energy in politics fused. Circumstances were ripe for Schurz in that the new national party needed a spokesman who could provide an entering wedge among foreign-born voters. Thus, existing condi-tions, as well as his own determination, account for his rise.

Schurz began his career as a Republican campaigner in 1856,

and in 1857 his race for the office of lieutenant governor of Wisconsin saw him narrowly defeated, possibly by the Know-Nothing vote. He was already in demand as a speaker at political rallies throughout the Middle West, and was forced to sandwich in his addresses on the fee-paying lyceum circuit as best he could. In 1859, Schurz spoke in Boston on the subject of equal rights for naturalized citizens at the invitation of local liberal Republicans who had opposed the Two-Year Amendment. As a result of his dispassionate analysis of American principles and traditions, Schurz became a celebrity in New England. Simultaneously, his lecture tours against the expansion of slavery, in which he discussed moral, constitutional, and economic factors in the growing national crisis before both German and American audiences, helped mold and harden public opinion in the North.

Schurz briefly attended the "Deutsches Haus" conference in which German Republicans caucused and organized convention strategy, but he was adamantly opposed to ethnic political separatism. At the Republican convention itself, where he presided over his state delegation, he shaped the plank on equal rights for all citizens. He, like most of the Germans, had favored Seward but accepted Lincoln's nomination, and thus won the scorn of militants like Heinzen. Thereafter, Schurz served on the Executive Committee of the party, reaching out to various nationality groups. After incessant whistle-stop campaign tours, he was rewarded by Lincoln with the post of American minister to Spain.[70]

Schurz thrived on applause and praise, and his letters to his wife exude cockiness and self-interest. He often wondered if he should have followed his original vocational choice, that of a professor "in a quiet setting," but his temperament and tastes precluded that option. Accusations that he was a self-seeker, made by militant and resentful Germans who charged him with becoming merely an American politician, do not reflect the full picture. Although Schurz pursued his own career ceaselessly and although he did drift away from former revolutionary contacts, he never became a docile party man. He hewed a strictly independent line, seeking to reform and streamline policies and procedures. Upon occasion, he became a forthright critic of his party, even breaking with it over the 1872 renomination of Grant and joining with the Liberal Republicans. In his career after the Civil War, as a Senator from Missouri and as Secretary of the Interior in the Hayes administration, Schurz stood for civil service reform, integrity in office, anti-imperialism, resource conservation, and sound money. He promoted various measures whether or not the Republican party supported them. While opportunism and a taste for power undoubtedly affected him, he acted as a reformer in politics.

Schurz was the patron saint of the Germans among the Forty-eighters, but his career was essentially American. His effort to influence the moral and intellectual direction of the German community expired with the slavery issue. His focus widened and the immigrant phase of his life ended there.[71]

After the Civil War, the Forty-eighters were a changed group. Some had abandoned activism, others had died, and many had modified their views. Most of them had adopted styles and pursuits that they had not anticipated. They served for a short time to bring Old World revolutionary visions to bear on New World problems, but all of them were inexorably absorbed by the new environment.

CHAPTER IV

Radical Labor

ONE GENERATION AFTER THE CIVIL WAR AN ALMOST IMPER-
ceptible change occurred in immigration to the United States.
Prior to the 1880's, immigration rolls had been composed
nearly exclusively of English, Irish, Scandinavians, and Germans. In the eighties, however, large numbers of immigrants
began to enter the United States from Eastern and Southern
Europe and, by century's end, southeastern Europeans dominated the statistics.[1]

Driven out by economic and social changes which undermined the traditional peasant economy, they were unprepared
by their agrarian and handicraft backgrounds for the impersonal,
urban-industrial milieu of the United States. These late nineteenth-century immigrants were in appearance, attitudes, and
mores different from the earlier immigrant groups. Their dress
and languages seemed to native Americans bizarre. Their
religions, Roman Catholic, Orthodox, or Jewish, almost never
Protestant, appeared exotic and, as a result, unwelcome. Because
of these attributes, the newcomers were viewed, at best, as
novel. They became known as the New Immigrants in contrast to the so-called Old Immigrants from Western Europe.[2]

These newcomers flocked into industries in which mechanization had succeeded in eliminating the necessity of training or
talent. In mines, mills, and factories, the new immigrants
displaced the old immigrants who, in turn, experienced upward
mobility into supervisory or managerial ranks, or entered
developing industries. English, Scottish, Welsh, Irish, and
German were gradually supplanted by Slovak, Magyar, Polish,
Italian, and Jewish workers. For the latter group, upward

[97]

mobility was unlikely, other than within the working class or within their own ethnic institutional network.[3]

A most significant fact about the wave of new immigration was its concurrence with the great leap forward into maturity of American industry. The industrial pace of the country quickened after the Civil War with the disappearance of the antebellum agrarian domination of the economy and the uneven pattern of wartime industrial growth. Climbing industrial indices became commonplace. Railroad mileage, coal, steel, petroleum, and even electrical consumption, and the manufacture of consumer goods all expanded throughout the last decades of the nineteenth century. In the various basic industries, technical changes and increased mechanization completed the decades-old evolution of a permanent class of wage earners. The scope and speed of large-scale industrialization diminished prospects of the worker becoming an independent capitalist or even a skilled tradesman in an emergent industry. Instead he was destined to be without a calling or career. As workers who were least likely to have capital or opportunities, the new immigrants became what one historian has labeled America's "forced labor" whose energy alone made possible the emergence of this nation as a world power. Without this crucial element, the phenomenal industrial expansion of the American economy in the late nineteenth century could not have occurred.[4]

In these decades, the organized labor movement began to assume both permanence and a degree of stability. As the movement crystallized, the attitude toward the new immigrants streaming into the country in the last years of the century was ambiguous, then fearful, and finally, hostile. The unions for the most part had come to adopt the British practice of organization by craft or trade rather than organization by industry. The result of such restrictiveness was a limited base: "labor" came to mean the skilled.[5] In addition, organized labor had moved away from its antebellum tendency to participate in social reform movements. Reform unionism, as it has been called, had characterized workers' organizations, especially the

Knights of Labor, earlier in the nineteenth century. But by the end of the eighties, the organized labor movement had abandoned its interest in social reforms in favor of concrete, bread-and-butter issues. It was narrowly dedicated to the pursuit of only the immediate goals of its own members without explicit reference to the needs of the unorganized.

The Knights of Labor was a national industrial federation which flourished in the seventies and into the eighties. The Knights aspired to achieve independent status for all workers regardless of skill, sex, or race. They were grounded in traditional democratic egalitarianism characteristic of the Jacksonian Era and, consequently, they refused to accept the decreasing importance of skills and the resulting insecurity. The industrialization that continued to undercut the value of crafts and trades was intolerable so long as the worker was reduced to helplessness. The Knights desired another social transformation which would restore worker autonomy. They opposed monopoly and the existing financial structure, favored labor self-help efforts including cooperative ventures, and supported political activism. They enjoyed the flexibility of such varied tactics, while lacking a firm strategy for change. But time and other factors served to undermine the Order, as the Knights' reformism "...did not harmonize with their environment...." Technological change mercilessly invalidated the Knights' dream and encouraged the evolution of a rival organization, the American Federation of Labor.

The A.F. of L. recognized the permanence of the wage-earner status of its members. The immigrant background of many of the leaders meant that they easily sidestepped the unrealistic ambition of native Americans to regain independence for individual workers. To some extent, A.F. of L. leaders tended toward a class view of society. Their aim was to secure practical gains for organized workers. They did not launch antimonopolistic or other reform campaigns and even eschewed the political stump. The efforts of these union leaders were bent toward developing the potential economic power of their members within the existing system. Thus, organized labor's heavily old-immigrant leadership abandoned the radical path of earlier native labor leaders for a more conservative and pragmatic route.[6]

Clearly, organized labor did not address itself directly to the exploited and neglected immigrant. Labor triumphs which happened to aid the immigrant were not so intended. The exclusive, minority labor movement offered nothing to these vulnerable workers and, indeed, the A.F. of L. eventually joined with nativists in the restrictionist campaign. Leadership for immigrant workers and attention to their concerns would have to emerge from their own ranks. They would have to help themselves because American society, which depended on their muscle, would not assist them. The extent of their struggle for survival is a little-known and often obscured segment of American labor and immigration history.

One of the most familiar instances of assertive action by immigrant workers in the latter part of the nineteenth century is, perhaps unfortunately, the episode of the Molly Maguires. This was not so much an example of self-help group action as of Irish quasi-secret societies involved in personal feuds and anti-employer terrorism in the Pennsylvania anthracite fields. A trial in 1875-76 which somewhat exaggerated their adventures, resulted in mass hangings and the crushing of organized action by ethnic miners in the area.[7] However, in this period examples abound of immigrant solidarity and organizational efforts. These were sometimes confined to the new immigrants alone and at other times, they occurred in conjunction with older immigrant workers. Leadership seemed to be the key element required to infuse life into an immigrant movement. Where a militant voice addressed itself to their needs, the immigrants responded. Upon occasion, events themselves ignited an ethnic community. New immigrants supported unionization, strikes, and even pioneered in seeking imaginative solutions to their plight.

In 1874, in reaction against the suffering and unemployment

brought about by the depression, immigrant miners in the Hocking Valley in Ohio organized a union and conducted a strike for over two months before they were defeated by the importation of black strikebreakers from cities in the border states and the South. The solidarity demonstrated by these Irish, Welsh, English, German, and Yankee miners immediately found an echo in other immigrant miners in Braidwood, Illinois. There, a more diverse miner population, which included Swedes, Italians, Poles, and Russians, as well as those nationalities represented in the Hocking Valley, formed a union and carried on a successful strike for fourteen weeks.

Throughout this period in various northeastern states, Italians organized their own separatist locals of masons, hodcarriers, and stonecutters, often as a reaction to the segregationist policies of the A.F. of L. Slavic anthracite miners in Pennsylvania played a significant role in the survival and growth of the United Mine Workers. In New York City, Philadelphia, Baltimore, and other urban centers where Russian Jews settled in the eighties, organizational efforts became commonplace. In these instances and many others, need and leadership joined in creating solidarity in a common cause. While it is indisputable that some immigrants of the various nationalities served as scabs and strikebreakers, the organizability of immigrant workers and their determined pursuit of positive goals can no longer be doubted.[8]

The alienation and disorganization experienced by the new immigrants—often responsible for their acceptance of the status quo—have been overemphasized by historians. While the hardships inherent in emigration and acculturation ought not to be ignored, for many immigrants social disorientation was minimized by the fact that they settled in groups, and thus often lived with the same neighbors in the New World as in the Old Country, especially if they settled in small towns.

The immigrant was apt to define himself primarily as a member of a family or a community, rather than in terms of his own individuality, and if economic pressures caused the group to take action, group consciousness invariably called forth solidarity. Thus, the social structure of the immigrant communities tended to impose conformity upon their members, and when such pressures were brought to bear upon industrial warfare, the immigrant could be a more tenacious labor loyalist than the Yankee individualist. The basis of such a posture was traditional, but the result was cohesive resistance and militancy. "In a strike, change was his goal, and his methods were radical," has been remarked about these immigrants. Another historian adds that "they were effective strikers because they were peasants."[9]

It has been acknowledged that immigrants offered political support for Progressive Era reforms based on their own self-interest, despite their image as dupes or allies of machine bosses.[10] It is now clear that in the economic arena immigrants were often vigorous fighters in the promotion of changes necessary for their survival. In the various industries in which they toiled, these immigrants responded to aggressive leadership when it appeared. Following is a consideration of the history of some of these immigrant workers and, where possible, the careers of selected immigrant radical leaders.

Miners and Millworkers

The immigrant groups throughout the nineteenth and in the beginning of the twentieth century who entered the mining pits of the United States were the English, Scottish, Welsh, Irish, and Germans of the old immigration and the Slavs, Magyars, and Italians of the new immigration. They contributed with pick and shovel to the dark underside of American industry. The English, however, stand out as the dominant group in the field, even late in the century, when immigration statistics from England to the United States indicate that the numbers of newcomers had dropped.

The Welsh and English made up the bulk of the Pennsylvania anthracite mineworkers after the 1820's, with the Scottish and English tending to dominate the bituminous minefields in western Pennsylvania, Maryland, West Virginia, the Midwest, and the Far West. Immigrants from the British Isles, with the exception of the Irish, often came as experienced miners whose Old Country background as coal hewers and ore diggers enabled them to play primary roles in the opening of new areas to mining. By the 1870's British miners occupied positions as foremen and superintendents in pits across the country.[11]

Conditions in American mines, where safety legislation came a generation after the British regulations of the forties, were precarious. Poor ventilation, flimsy supports, and other hazards led to higher accident rates in American mines and pressured discontented miners into seeking ways to ameliorate conditions. Reinforcement was provided for the English miners by the knowledge of the independent political activities conducted by coal miners in England. There, miners campaigned and elected their own representatives to the House of Commons. As a result, miners here sought to follow their own political path in this country. In addition, they emulated the example of British and Scottish miners who set up cooperatively owned stores in order to avoid dependence on the company store.[12]

Some of the coal miners had been involved in labor organizations in England, some even emigrating as a result of blacklisting, and thus Englishmen organized the first unions in the Pennsylvania anthracite fields before the Civil War. In soft-coal mining, too, before and after the war, English miners initiated unionist activity in Maryland, Illinois, and other mining areas. Englishmen dominated the leadership of the Miners' and Laborers' Benevolent Association which in the early seventies had several branches in eastern Pennsylvania and conducted organizational agitation and strikes. Many of these activists joined hands to form the abortive Miners' National Association of the United States in 1873. English miners were prominent in the formation of the United Mine Workers in 1890, and the union's popular and influential president, John Mitchell, was a first-generation son of Orange Irish parents, reared in the Scottish and English mining village of Braidwood, Illinois.[13]

These English-dominated miners' unions were among the few American unions to allow their leadership to run for political office. In contrast to the policy of the A.F. of L., to which the U.M.W. belonged, workers themselves were encouraged to become involved in politics in order to achieve improved conditions, stronger bargaining positions, and even the nationalization of mines. Interest in a labor party was frequently voiced. By the eighties when those from the British Isles were abandoning work in the mines to the less skilled new immigrants, English leadership and policies in the emerging unions had solidified.[14]

The Germans and the Irish often followed the English into influential positions in the miners' unions, since these two ethnic groups entered the mines on the heels of the English and Scottish workers. By century's end they shared leadership of the polyglot groups that made up the work force in the industry. In Illinois, one of the earliest mining areas to experience organization and strike activity, was located the most radical branch of the United Mine Workers. It was heavily influenced by a German immigrant worker, named Adolph Germer (1881-1966), who persuaded the membership to continue third-party political activity following the demise of Populism in the late nineties.[15]

Adolph Germer emigrated to the United States as a child and began work in the coal fields of central Illinois at the age of ten. He apparently was influenced by the German-speaking radical movement of Cook County, and spent decades in labor and radical circles, ending his career, however, as a conservative influence in the C.I.O. In the first fifteen years of the twentieth century, Germer provided the link between the Illinois branch of the U.M.W. and the Socialist party.

Within the labor movement, he sought to propel the A.F. of L. toward greater acceptance of industrial unionism. Through his efforts in concert with a few other organizers, the United Mine Workers in Illinois reached out to the militant Western Federation of Miners, despite its departure from the A.F. of L.

After the turn of the century, however, when the western faction of the miners' movement began to demonstrate syndicalist tendencies, with an increasing emphasis on economic rather than political action, Germer opposed that trend and sought personally to diminish the influence of Big Bill Haywood, leader of the Industrial Workers of the World. In his political efforts, Germer encouraged an alliance between the miners and the Socialists. He himself ran on the Socialist ticket for the Illinois legislature, he obtained party funds for miners' strikes, and he eventually assumed national office in the Socialist party. He bent all his efforts 'toward convincing the working miner that socialism offered him the brightest promise.

Germer was a gentle person, a trait clearly evident in the bitter controversies that racked the radical movements of his time. His radicalism stemmed from his devotion to the cause of the exploited miner, whose difficult life Germer knew intimately, rather than theoretically. Germer was convinced that the only hope for miners lay in the nationalization of the mines. This seemed self-evident to him, but in order to convince workers to this view, he trod cautiously He opposed the general strike as a tactic difficult to implement and likely to frighten potential converts. He chose instead to rely on political action. Miners and other workers must exercise their vote to elect socialists who, once in public office, would seek to institute nationalization of the mines and other heavy industries.[16]

In the Mountain States in the last decades of the nineteenth century, the typical miner was a native American but some of his leaders were immigrants from England or Ireland. Conditions were even more onerous for the miners in the West than for their Eastern comrades, and thus there was greater impetus toward aggressive action as a means of survival. Economic growth resulting in corporate concentration and the separation of ownership and management occurred rapidly in the West, creating a strong sense of alienation and helplessness in the workers. Such alienation against a background of hitherto loose frontier conditions eventually brought workers together in solidarity and militant unionism. Extremely repressive tactics by mining operators and the state governments, which the mining interests often controlled, solidified those impulses. Thus, environmental pressures rather than imported radical notions seem clearly to have been at work.[17]

Nonetheless, foreign-born leadership was noticeable in the evolution of the most radical union in the Western states, the Western Federation of Miners. Edward Boyce (1863-1941), who served as W.F.M. president from 1896 to 1902, was one of the founders and the primary force in the increasing radicalism of the union in its first decade. Boyce, like Germer, was a workingman. He emigrated to the United States from Ireland at the age of twenty. As a penniless laborer he wandered over the country, and in the mines of Colorado in 1884 embarked upon his union career. Familiar with exploitation, he reached for any tactic which might improve mine conditions, joining a miners' local affiliated with the Knights of Labor, serving as a Populist in the Colorado legislature, and accepting membership briefly in the A.F. of L. By 1897, early in his presidency of the Federation, Boyce had transcended these tentative efforts and made a determined commitment to a two-pronged strategy of militant industrial unionism and socialist politics [18]

Boyce's industrial unionism encompassed all workers, regardless of skill, race, or nationality. With the exception of the oriental immigrant, he aimed for complete worker solidarity and unity as the first step toward eliminating the American worker's helplessness. In order to push American labor as a whole to a more militant posture, he took the W.F.M. out of the A.F. of L., and organized the rival Western Labor Union, a separate labor federation in the shadow of his own union. Boyce moved continually left, and by 1900, after the collapse of Populism, he advised the metal miners to support Socialist Eugene Debs at the ballot box and to organize themselves politically. Boyce had come to accept a Marxist analysis of society. The capitalist system itself and not wages and hours were the issue. He told the miners in convention:

There are only two classes of people in this world: one is composed of men and women who produce all; the other composed of men and women who produce nothing. . . . the time has arrived when this organization should array itself upon the side of the producers and advise its members to take political action and work for the adoption of those principles that are destined to free the people from the grasp of the privileged classes. . . .

Conditions had made strikes and boycotts ineffectual and, thus, those weapons had to be supplemented, first, with arms for self-defense, Boyce said, and secondly, with ballots marked for Socialist candidates. His rhetoric of resistance and confrontation suggested French syndicalism, but his major emphasis on politics negated it. Political rather than economic methods were the primary means to uplift the workers, and in 1902 a committee report submitted during the tenth annual convention of the Western Federation of Miners declared its goals to be public ownership of the means of production and distribution and the abolition of the wage system. The convention, more cautious, recommended only that its locals endorse the Socialist party.[19]

With the retirement of Boyce from the union presidency, the W.F.M. had completed its formative phase and its grounding in radicalism. His successors among the leadership, native Americans Charles H. Moyer and Big Bill Haywood, sought to build on the militant framework Boyce had erected. But in the next decade the union followed a curious path in which it fathered the Wobblies in 1905 and yet by 1911 returned quietly to the fold of the A.F. of L. However unique its meanderings, its early odyssey can be explained in terms of the Western experience. Late nineteenth-century social polarization had prepared the miners for radical leadership which arrived with the elevation to the union presidency of Ed Boyce, an Irish immigrant with a keen sense of outrage and a determined quest for justice.

Paralleling the Irish-inspired militancy among the miners was the solidarity and unity of the new immigrant textile workers in the East. Several new immigrant nationality groups worked in the polluted environment of the New England and New Jersey textile mills, and in 1912 and 1913 in two widely publicized strikes, they went out against intolerable conditions and wage cuts. Frozen out of the United Textile Workers, a skilled union affiliated with the A.F. of L., the unskilled immigrants appealed for support and leadership to the Wobblies who at once joined the battle.[20]

The Wobblies saw themselves as the champions of the neglected unskilled migrants and immigrants, and thus, a symbiotic relationship easily crystallized during the textile strikes. Specifically, the industrial federation, since its founding in 1905, had sought to reach those workers who were economically and socially marginal to American society. The Wobblies offered assistance, camaraderie, and self-respect as well as a revolutionary ideology which combined primitive millennarianism and Marxist analysis. I.W.W. tactics of direct action were clear and logical to the southern and eastern European immigrants who turned to the Wobblies: striking, boycotting, and sabotaging production were effective or at least more immediate than signing ironclad contracts or organizing political campaigns.[21]

The Wobbly leadership was for the most part native American. The background of Big Bill Haywood, originally a miner in the West and a one-time protegé of Ed Boyce in the W. F. M., was characteristic of those former workers who made up the leadership of the I. W. W. Yet there were many immigrants in the organization whose formative experiences in industrial relations had taken place in the European labor movement. The first Secretary-Treasurer of the I. W. W. was William E. Trautmann, born in New Zealand of German parentage and active in the socialist and labor movements in Germany and Russia before emigrating to the United States. James Larkin, an organizer for the Wobblies, had been a labor leader in the Emerald Isle before coming to the United States and joining the I.W.W. Another Irishman who was active in both Irish and American radical circles was James Connolly, who propagandized and organized for the Wobblies in their early years before he returned to Ireland and to martyrdom in the Easter Rebellion of 1916.

The new immigrants had their own ethnic representatives among the Wobbly organizers and agitators. Joseph Ettor (1886-1948), an ironworker, exemplified the new immigrant as labor activist. He was born to an Italian immigrant family in Brooklyn, and plied his trade alongside other immigrants. Awakened early to social inequities, he became an organizer for the Wobblies in several different languages and on both coasts.[22]

Lawrence, Massachusetts, one of the most ethnically cosmopolitan cities in the country, was founded as a textile center in 1845 and rapidly became the industry's capital in the United States. The 85,000 residents of the town in 1912 looked to the textile mills, especially to the dominant American Woolen Company, for their primary means of support. Perhaps half the population over the age of fourteen earned its livelihood in the mills. A large proportion of these workers were new immigrants.

Historically, the mills of Massachusetts had always depended on uprooted, migrant labor. First, native American rural girls entered mill work in order to earn their dowries, and thereafter each of the immigrant groups in turn tended the spinning and weaving machinery. The Irish and Germans were followed by the French-Canadians, and in the nineties, by the new immigrants. At the end of the first decade of the twentieth century, the mill workers lived packed in tenements which were among the most crowded in the nation. By day they worked in the dust, moisture, and humidity of the mills and were pressured to operate mutiple machines under the watchful stare of foremen who often undercounted their piecework. The cumulative effect could be read in a high accident and mortality rate. Wages had climbed and hours had been decreased over the decades, but the life of the mill worker remained oppressive.[23]

In January, 1912, the Italian, Franco-Belgian, Polish, Syrian, and Jewish workers, accompanied by some of the Germans and Lithuanians, struck over short pay envelopes following a state-ordered reduction of the work week from fifty-six to fifty-four hours. Following the direction of grass-roots leaders, such as the teen-age worker Angelo Rocco, and ignoring clerical advice to acquiesce, they summoned Joe Ettor, known through the small Italian I.W.W. local in town. Ettor was accompanied by the anarchist poet and mystic Arturo Giovanitti. Giovanitti (1884-1959) had emigrated from Italy in 1900. At the time of the Lawrence strike, he was the editor and publisher of a syndicalist newspaper called *Il Proletario,* and was regarded among Italian-Americans as a romantic revolutionary. In his paper he emphasized revolutionary direct action on behalf of the working masses. Ettor and Giovanitti, with other Wobblies, led the 23,000 immigrant strikers to success in eight weeks.

While the heterogeneous immigrant groups lacked the background of common union experience, their ethnic institutional networks sufficed. For example, their ethnic bands played at demonstrations, their charities provided relief funds to the strikers, and their newspapers supplied encouragement. This network of support was crucial in sustaining the strike effort. Management, which had the support of the municipal government, the old immigrant skilled workers, and their union, provoked violence and succeeded in jailing Ettor and Giovanitti, but finally surrendered in the face of a device adopted from strikers in Europe: in a well-publicized move, the strikers' children were evacuated for their protection beyond the strike zone to sympathetic families in New York, Philadelphia, and Jersey City.

National attention led to a congressional hearing. The public proved sympathetic; the strikers won the argument and their slim pay envelopes thickened somewhat. Moreover, they had demonstrated their militancy in industrial conflict behind avowedly radical labor leaders. Also these heterogeneous peoples had shown that despite their differing social structures and parochial backgrounds, they could coalesce behind a mutual goal. For the Wobblies, the result was the establishment of a beachhead on the East Coast as the mill workers signed up with the radical industrial union. It was a fleeting triumph, however, as management gradually weeded out the strike leaders and the union members, and soon most of the workers deserted the union. But during the crisis, these neglected workers, ignored by the conservative labor movement, had devised their own strategies, secured leadership, and utilized family and community strengths, thus improving their conditions.[24]

An encore occurred the next year, although the drama had a different conclusion. In another grim, one-industry town, new immigrant millworkers acted against oppressive conditions and appealed to the Wobblies to help them achieve victory. Twenty-five thousand silk workers in Paterson, New Jersey, struck against the expansion of the multiple-loom system. As in Lawrence, the skilled workers held back and the United Textile Workers failed to confront the companies over the issue. Some English-speaking skilled workers did join the strike, but essentially it was another protest conducted by the unskilled, new immigrants. The I.W.W. provided assistance and suggested a stage pageant at Madison Square Garden in order to win national publicity. This ploy failed, however, proving to be too diversionary for the strikers. When the English-speaking workers caved in after six months, a settlement occurred with each of the companies involved. The new immigrants suffered defeat at Paterson, but their lines had held.[25]

Needle Workers

In the clothing industry the new immigrants pioneered in the creation of a new unionism renowned for its broad humanitarian and enlightened policies and based on ideals of social reconstruction. That such a progressive movement grew after the 1890's out of the chaotic garment industry, not yet mechanized or systematized, was the result of the background of the workers themselves. Their identity, traditions, and values explain the thrust of their movement even more than the oppressive sweatshop conditions or the fragmentation of the industry.

The great expansion of the ready-made clothing business coincided with the mass emigration from Eastern Europe. Instead of a factory system, contracting prevailed in the industry. By 1890 middlemen purchased cut materials from manufacturers. These contractors in turn hired workers at piece-rates who rented or purchased sewing machines and worked, often as a family unit, within the confines of tenement flats. Under such conditions, regulation was impossible and legislation meaningless. The garment workers labored sometimes eighty-four hours per week at subsistence wages under squalid, even disease-causing conditions. Neither industry stability nor seasonal insecurity deterred immigrants from taking up positions at sewing machines since the simple steps of each stage of garment production required little skill or training.[26]

These new immigrants moved into various areas of the trade formerly dominated by Germans. The bulk of the workers streaming into the garment industry in New York City and other East Coast industrial centers was Jewish. These immigrants, along with numbers of Italian workers, had come to the United States without an apprenticeship in European factories. Their experience was in handicrafts and village commerce, and was not relevant to the urban-industrial complex. However, their communal traditions, above average educational level, and economic need prepared these immigrants to unite against exploitative conditions. Moreover, emerging Jewish social services and religious institutions endowed the community with more cohesiveness than many other groups possessed. Most of these immigrants wished merely to survive and compete, and one day to become garment contractors. But beside them in the sweatshops were radical intellectuals, political refugees whose formative experiences had occurred in the labor movement in Russia, culminating in the Bund, the Jewish workers' organization. Mutual hardships in the sweatshops of America bred an atmosphere of trust, and after the Russian-speaking intellectuals learned Yiddish, the language of the Jewish masses, they were able to assume leadership of the garment workers. A supportive role was played by Italian workers who, despite their Catholicism, less stable migratory pattern, and a relatively weak institutional structure, accepted the leadership of radical intellectuals among them.[27]

Industry conditions mitigated against the emergence of successful labor organization, and it was not until the twentieth century that strong unions evolved. But an undercurrent of union solidarity gradually developed· while on the surface factionalism and doctrinaire disputes flared among the intellectuals whose allegiances were divided among anarchism, Marxism, and the socialism of Daniel DeLeon's Socialist Labor party. In 1900 sufficient support existed for the founding of the International Ladies' Garment Workers' Union, a federation of semi-industrial unions of unskilled and semi-skilled workers. The organization encompassed seven unions in four East Coast cities, represented two thousand workers, and affiliated with the A.F. of L.[28]

At the end of its first decade, the I.L.G.W.U. became entrenched in the industry through two general strikes involving thousands of workers. Late in 1909, twenty thousand Jewish and Italian girls spontaneously walked off the job in protest against the long hours and the low wages. These waist and dressmakers, in the first great strike by women in American history, held out throughout the severe winter months, and eventually won a compromise settlement. The next summer a general strike called by the International resulted in the largest strike New York had ever seen. Fifty to sixty thousand cloak, suit, and skirt makers conducted a prolonged strike which altered the nature of industrial relations in the clothing industry and bore vast implications for labor and management throughout the nation. Both struggles had demonstrated the efficacy of the general strike in an atomized industry, and had shown not only that immigrants could be militant but that it was true of even a more neglected group, the immigrant working woman.[29]

The summer-long strike was settled resulting in worker gains in higher wages and shorter hours. But the real triumph lay in the signing of the so-called Protocol of Peace, pushed through by the influence of Louis D. Brandeis, and other prominent public personalities who participated in the negotiations. The preferential union shop was established as well as a Joint Board of Sanitary Control, a Board of Arbitration, and a Board of Grievances. "Despite evasion and ultimate breakdown, the Protocol, with employers, union, and public representatives accepting joint responsibility, explored new paths for industrial peace." The immigrants had succeeded in organizing the ladies' garment industry, and the International quickly expanded to a membership of 90,000. In 1914, with the formation of the Amalgamated Clothing Workers of America (outside the A. F. of L.) the men's clothing industry also became organized by militant immigrant tailors.[30]

Unlike other successful labor organizations, not one strong personality dominated the garment unions, but several colorful figures emerged from the ranks to leadership and, out of the community, influential immigrant lawyers and journalists offered guidance and support. Typifying internal leadership was I.L.G.W.U. president Benjamin Schlesinger (1876-1932) who headed the federation for many years. Schlesinger came to the United States from Lithuania in 1891, and found employment as a cloak and suit maker in the unorganized garment industry in Chicago. His emerging ideological convictions and his passion for widening workers' horizons and opportunities led him to become rapidly committed to the principle of organization.[31]

From descriptions by contemporaries, Schlesinger was apparently closer to an ethereal rabbinical student than to an organizer, but he spent his life moving easily between the harsh realities of unionism and Yiddish-language journalism. As a labor leader in Chicago and, later, in New York, he presided over the I.L.G.W.U. in its formative period. His was a dual influence in the movement. Schlesinger attempted to draw the garment workers to the organized socialists, an effort which once cost him his office during a factional struggle. Simultaneously, he bent his strength toward workers' needs, both immediate and long-range. He led locals of the I.L.G.W.U. to establish sick-benefit funds, he was influential in the implementation of the Joint Board of Sanitary Control, and he arranged for lectures and adult education courses for the membership. An apparent irascibility did not undercut his effective pursuit of union goals.[32]

A different kind of leadership was exemplified in Meyer London (1871-1926) whose work demonstrated the concentric forces present in the immigrant Jewish community. Through London's career the blending of the immigrant intellectual elite, the socialist ideology, and the community institutional network on behalf of the workers becomes clear. London was born in Poland and emigrated when he was twenty years old. He attended a law school in New York, and was admitted to the bar in 1898. By that date, he was immersed in Lower East Side issues and politics, and was participating in labor and socialist struggles. His commitment was more populist than Marxist, and he was neither manipulator nor theorist, but rather a humanitarian seeking the well-being of his community through unionization and politics.[33]

London served as a legal adviser to labor in both the women's and men's garment unions, as a counselor on union policy, and as a spokesman in negotiations with management. He could be conciliatory but his devotion to the workers made him tenacious in collective bargaining. He was determined to see the garment industry organized as a whole, rather than limited to the largest manufacturers, and it was London who successfully represented labor in the bargaining sessions which led to the Protocol of Peace in 1910.[34]

London's reward for his efforts was election on the Socialist ticket to the House of Representatives from New York's Twelfth District in 1914. There, he sought legislation to ease the lives of his worker-constituents and to gain for them a measure of security. As a member of the House Committee on Labor, he supported limitations on child labor, the extension of the eight-hour day, national unemployment and illness insurance, and old-age pensions. He also favored maternity allowances and opposed immigration restrictions. Serving in the Congress from 1914 to 1918, and again from 1920 to 1922, at the outbreak of the war he argued against American entry. He lectured his colleagues on the socialist view of war as an expression of economic conflict. He was the only member of the House to vote against the passage of the Espionage Act in 1917. During the war, he argued on behalf of the maintenance of civil liberties, and after the Armistice, he recommended a general amnesty for political prisoners and measures to prevent work dislocation in the transition to a peacetime economy.[35]

Other immigrant figures also played prominent roles of varying significance. A major socialist influence among the unions' legal advisers was Morris Hillquit, a national leader of the Socialist Party of America (see Chapter V). He and others solidified the commitment of these particular immigrant workers to forward-looking labor positions.[36]

The policies pursued by the garment unions revealed both the socialist perspective of the leadership and the cultural milieu of the membership. What emerged was a composite ethnic and ideological picture. A vibrant tradition of radicalism developed in the sweatshops and ghettos against the background of the membership's Eastern European hardships and persecution. Great sensitivity to oppression existed and resulted in a humanitarian and idealistic commitment to equality and justice. Undoubtedly the vital factor was collective memories rather than the Marxist ideology of some union officers.

The garment workers' unions supported political action, leading to a de facto alliance with the Socialist party before and after the First World War. In 1903 the I.L.G.W.U. in convention adopted a resolution commending the Socialist party to its membership. At the height of the era of progressive reformism, it did not fall in line with either Wilsonian reformers or the Progressive party of 1912. Instead, the I.L.G.W.U. in those years endorsed the idea of class consciousness and, while not formally aligned to the Socialist party, it supported various socialist candidates for public office. At A.F. of L. conventions garment workers' representatives promoted radical resolutions and encouraged industrial unionism. They favored unrestricted immigration, non-racist union policies, female suffrage, and welfare legislation. While some of the most vociferous members concentrated on fostering class consciousness and believed that the labor movement could revolutionize the social structure of the United States, the union nevertheless remained within the A.F. of L. and defended the Federation on the basis of having brought stability and benefits to working people. But within the confines of the conservative American labor movement, the immigrant garment workers' unions sponsored full educational programs, comprehensive welfare benefits, and the earliest union-run medical clinics in the country. Their illness and death benefits far surpassed those already familiar to American unionists, and were in fact suggestive of an all-encompassing movement which intimately touched the lives of all its members.[37]

The ideological stance of these immigrant unions received renewed impetus through the continuous arrival of Russian refugees, especially after the abortive Russian Revolution of 1905. That revolutionary strain, the nature of the industry, and the composition of the work force prolonged the radicalism of these semi-industrial garment unions well beyond the closing of the gates on immigration after the First World War.[38]

Various ethnic groups which comprised the new immigration contributed vigorously to the effort to achieve equitable conditions for working people in the United States. Whether in isolated mining locales, impoverished mill centers, or congested East Coast metropolises, the unskilled new immigrants wrote their own chapters in the history of the American labor movement. Burdened by singularly harsh economic and social pressures and usually ignored by the skilled trade unions, they were capable of presenting a solid front on the field of industrial warfare. New immigrants, unlike older Americans, were seldom propelled to action because of technical change undermining status or position. Rather, they were often radicalized when exploitative industrial factors ignited culturally shaped responses.

There is heavy irony in the fact that organized labor rejected the unskilled new immigrants because of their supposed passivity and lack of cohesiveness in industrial relations. Labor's pragmatic leadership accepted the existing social structure and wage-earner status, and strived to protect their selective gains. They ostracized the waves of New Immigrants, and transformed potential allies into rivals and even scabs. The unskilled were abandoned to a lonely struggle for survival. Isolated as they were, they created their own leadership, borrowed on their past experiences and values, and formulated their own strategies.

CHAPTER V

The Revolutionaries

THE VAST THRONGS OF IMMIGRANTS ARRIVING IN THE UNITED States between the close of the Civil War and the First World War included a number of politically conscious intellectuals who introduced new ideological strains into American society. These men and women had been brought up in an ambience of rigidity and inflexibility where legal channels for growth and change were either non-existent or extremely tenuous and narrow. To these alienated intellectuals, reform in Central and Eastern Europe was an impossibility. If those countries were to become equitable societies, the only option was revolution. But they were not sanguine about it.

Among the German radicals of the last decades of the nineteenth century, there was not even the optimism of the defeated Forty-eighters who had expected and hoped for a second and successful revolution. Rather, these later arrivals had been confronted by a unified and authoritarian German Reich under the iron rule of a chancellor who was capable of manipulating electoral mechanisms and civil liberties, forcing dissenters underground or into exile. Little hope existed of breaching the closed system. Among the Eastern European intellectuals, even less viability could be envisioned. In the Russian Empire, especially, autocracy still ruled, though it appeared to be weakening under the heavy weight of a cumbersome bureaucracy. In Russia, in the Austro-Hungarian Empire, and in the Balkans, secret conspiracies and organizations mushroomed, but the oppressive environment mitigated against success.

The frustration and despair of the intelligentsia of Eastern

Europe transformed what might have been liberalizing influences in their native societies into alienated revolutionary tendencies. When these people emigrated, they brought to the United States a much more pronounced class spirit characteristic of professional revolutionaries than had been present before. They also brought with them suggestions of force and violence new to the United States.

These immigrant radicals who settled in the expanding urban centers of the East and Midwest in the decades after the Civil War did not look upon the United States as a new nation. To these newcomers, the society in which they found themselves was not immature and unstructured. They, unlike antebellum immigrant reformers, did not view the nation as fertile for and hospitable to social experimentation. Rather than an undeveloped and flexible society waiting to be molded, the United States appeared to them to be structured and polarized. The entering intelligentsia immediately recognized the existence of a "social question" in American industrial conditions. While the dimensions and intensity of their appraisal of the United States were often distorted and heavily colored by their previous experiences, nevertheless they grasped intuitively the social and economic crises. The exploitation within the system persuaded them that the country was ripe not merely for reform but for revolution.

These radicals tried to reach out to the immigrant worker. He was the natural object of their attention, for his unexpectedly harsh social experiences in the Promised Land were suggestive of the Old Country which he had fled. Moreover, he was "relatively lacking in what might be called a traditional American ideology."[1] So it appeared to the immigrant revolutionaries.

Out of the materials of their own lives and the urban-industrial milieu which they encountered, these immigrant revolutionaries formulated political paths new to the United States. Between the decades of Reconstruction and the First World War, they built revolutionary movements based upon ideas which they themselves had imported.

The Socialists

Scientific or Marxist socialism became the most notorious of all the radical ideologies imported by immigrants to the United States. Influential qualitatively more than quantitatively, scientific socialism impressed itself upon the American consciousness in the last decades of the nineteenth century and the first two decades of the twentieth century. It captured the loyalty of numbers of immigrant intellectuals and workers before the turn of the century, and subsequently dazzled enough native-born citizens to form a movement in American accents. Ultimately the American government and the public at large reacted in alarm greater than they had demonstrated to any earlier foreign doctrine.

Unlike earlier collectivist ideologies of various utopian shadings, Marxism sought to transform society rather than to build new communities outside the old. Distinct from anarchist collectivism, which strived to demolish the system at one stroke, Marxist socialism expected to exploit existing strains and tendencies and to build a new society from the shell of the old. The first manifestation of a Marxist organization of identifiable strength and influence has been singled out by the socialist leader and historian Morris Hillquit as the General German Labor Association, founded in New York City in 1869.[2]

The international socialist movement evolving in various Western countries in the last third of the nineteenth century struggled to define its principles and strategies within the theories of Karl Marx. In the United States, too, socialists of different stripes attempted to sort themselves out. Excluding the anarchists who chose their own separatist path at their congress in 1883, the socialists were divided into a faction which emphasized economic tactics and another which stressed political methods. In accord with the vacillation traditional in American labor circles, genuine conflict arose over the tactics to be used in furthering the class struggle—whether to support primarily labor organizations or political parties.

The socialists who adhered closely to Marx believed in utilizing labor organizations. Through unionization and confrontation with capital, workers would develop class consciousness and, thereafter, would gravitate to political action and the eventual capture of political power. An opposing view, held by socialists who followed the teachings of Ferdinand Lassalle, founder of the socialist movement in Germany, emphasized the direct political path to power. Unionism was dismissed as an unnecessary detour en route to worker control of the state. These contradictory tendencies were pitted against each other while the socialists simultaneously sought to win support from workers who themselves drifted continually from political to economic programs.[3]

The Marxist movement in the United States began almost two decades before 1869, the date which Hillquit cites. Prior to the Civil War through the organizational efforts and teachings of Joseph Weydemeyer, and thereafter, through the work of his successor, Friedrich A. Sorge (1827-1906), Marxism was a consistent thread in the fabric constituting the labor movement. Sorge, born in Saxony, was imbued with liberal values and revolutionary sympathies through his father, a Lutheran minister. At the age of twenty-one, young Sorge participated in the armed conflicts of 1848-1849 in Saxony, Baden, and the Palatinate. With the collapse of the revolution, he moved from Germany to Switzerland, and then to Belgium and London, supporting himself as a music teacher, while involved in German radical circles. In 1852 he took up residence in the United States and, five years later, became politically active through membership in the newly organized Communist Club of New York, an educational society.[4]

For a few years he supported amorphous reformist causes; he moved from an antireligious orientation to the democratic radicalism of Heinzen, and only in 1866 did he become an avowed Marxist propagandist. For the next dozen years, Sorge embodied Marxism in America, until his retirement from activism to journalism. Sorge's Communist Club became a section of the International Workingmen's Association in 1867, then dividing into Marxist, Lassallean, and Bakuninist factions. When in 1872 the seat of the International was transferred by Marx and Engels from London to New York as a means of minimizing Bakuninist influences, Sorge became the general secretary of the International. He managed to breathe life into the dying organization for an additional four years.[5]

Sorge attempted to win support for the International from the all-inclusive and unstable National Labor Union, which endured a brief, precarious existence in the late sixties. The N.L.U., evolving toward a political emphasis which clashed with the Marxist economic approach, never officially established a tie to the International. At the same time, however, the General German Labor Association in New York, basically Lassallean, joined with Sorge and his comrades to organize a reform-minded political party, and soon thereafter affiliated with the International. These isolated episodes indicate the ideological imprecision of the Marxists in America as well as the difficulty in attracting Americans to European socialist doctrines. Those native Americans who joined sections of the International tended to be few and individualist, even eccentric, such as Virginia Woodhull and Tennessee Claflin. Sexual freedom advocates, they were eventually expelled for their wide-ranging political and social reformism.[6]

Sorge assumed control of an organization whose American branch consisted of several nationality sections; it was confined mainly to New York and Chicago and was composed of Germans, French, Bohemians, and infrequently Americans. He strove to intensify centralization, and he successfully presided over the appearance of new sections in various midwestern cities of large German populations. In 1874 the International held a national convention in Philadelphia which went on record as supporting political action only when a labor party was sufficiently strong to influence the political process. Until such a time, the emphasis was to be placed upon the economic sphere, with political activity confined to the pursuit of legislative measures in the interests of the workers. The firm enunciation of the primacy of the economic struggle became the last act of the International in America. With the onset of the fierce depression of the seventies, workers turned to political action as a panacea. Factionalism appeared in the International and, with the inability of reform-minded Americans to accept the discipline as well as the class and economic orientation of the Marxists, Sorge led a congress of the International to a declaration of its own worldwide demise.[7]

During his period of leadership, he demonstrated a greater understanding of American conditions than had many other radical immigrants. Sorge insisted on the necessity of reaching out to American workers while he simultaneously recognized their individualist attitudes. In his only English-language article, he stressed the liberty and justice which socialism represented, and he minimized the possibility of destructiveness and disorder. Knowing his American audience, he emphasized the evolutionary route to the new order as well as respect for existing social institutions, such as the family and personal property. He argued that common interests and collective forms were emerging from established traditions and that expropriation, when it occurred, would be accepted by all in the interest of humanity. His formula remained that of worker solidarity through organization but, despite his reassuring and placid tones, the Marxist movement remained in the hands of the foreign-born.[8]

The decade of the eighties saw the Marxists in the United States wandering in their own special wilderness. Theoretically, those tumultuous years offered inviting opportunities for any group of dissenters who represented alternate solutions to the discontented. The fragmentation of the Knights of Labor, the slow emergence of the American Federation of Labor, the uneven pace of the eight-hour movement, and the bloodletting of the Haymarket affair occurred while Marxists were unable to take advantage of events because of their own policy confusion and their pronounced lack of leadership. Instead of growth, there was stagnation, instead of direction, indecision. While they managed to organize a national party in 1876, an official cautioned against unrealistic optimism: "Let us not conceal the truth: the Socialist Labor Party is only a German colony. . . ."[9]

The Socialist Labor party, becoming distinct from the anarchists, went on record as hostile to armed action. A number of socialist journals sprang up and became aligned with the party, including one English-language newspaper, the *Workmen's Advocate*. But alongside of such signs of determination and vigor, weakness and internal division persisted. The party pursued political action, for example, in its support for Henry George in the mayoralty election in New York City in 1886. But it remained unresolved as to whether its purpose was propaganda or legislation. Its trade-union policy of "boring from within" was not impressively successful, as organized labor continued to accept modern industrial capitalism and therefore the need to advance its own interests within that structure. The S.L.P. after a dozen years lay hopelessly divided between a political faction and a trade-union faction which condemned the party to constant tactical reversals. Finally, a titan emerged whose dominance of the party endured, though challenged, for a generation.[10]

He was Daniel DeLeon (1852-1914) who was born in Curaçao but settled in New York at the age of twenty. His family sent him to Europe for his education, and thereafter he earned a law degree at Columbia University. He dabbled in various reform issues while pursuing a teaching career. His interest in social conditions drove him from supporting the Henry George campaign to the Edward Bellamy utopian socialist movement, then to the Socialist Labor party. The S.L.P. became his lifetime career.

Through his own forceful personality DeLeon assumed control of the S.L.P. shortly after joining the party in 1889. He shaped and energized the amorphous organization into a cohesive instrument to which he applied his own Marxist views. Overnight it became the center of revolutionary focus. As the brilliant DeLeon himself was responsible for the party's sudden flowering, he was also the cause of its fading. His unrestrained rhetorical invective, his insistence upon his own version of Marxist doctrine, and the value he placed upon principles, but never upon individuals, brought interminable divisions to the movement. The intolerance of a Karl Heinzen withers by comparison with the zealotry of DeLeon's emphasis on unquestioned party discipline.[11]

DeLeon resolved the Marxist-Lassallean dichotomy within the S.L.P. and moved the party squarely into the camp of Marxist doctrine. Indeed, in the face of Marxist revisionism, which was beginning to engulf the international socialist movement, DeLeon and his party adhered to a nearly unaltered and increasingly isolated orthodoxy. The ideological modifications that he made in later years were unrelated to European socialist revisionism.

DeLeon believed that the irrepressible class struggle, stemming from the inexorable movement of objective economic conditions, would inevitably result in social revolution. Anticipating Lenin, he wrote that the workers would be organized and educated by an elitist vanguard, "the head of the column," to which was assigned the task of imbuing the masses with a sense of class. When indoctrination was completed, workers would vote for socialism and, through their strategic economic location, would assume control of the means of production and distribution. Thus, unions would carry out an electoral mandate for socialism but little dislocation or show of force was expected to be necessary.

The weapons which were to be employed during the class struggle were both political and economic, DeLeon taught. The revolution must be encouraged in both arenas. He endorsed political action in order to stimulate agitation and education. Political means were never to be utilized to secure ameliorative legislation or to capture office within the capitalist system; DeLeon held in great contempt parliamentarian socialists and their gradualist path to the new order. Political action was prized essentially for its propaganda value.

He also admitted the need for economic action. Labor solidarity on an industry-wide basis, rather than through isolated unions and sporadic strikes or boycotts, was to him the proper method of confronting emerging corporations. The "New Trade

Unionism," as DeLeon labeled his approach, represented, in its full theoretical development, revolutionary industrial unionism. A federation of industrial unions of all workers would insure the complete triumph of the working class. These industrial "constituencies" would form the basis of the socialist republic as the state disappeared.[12]

From his position as editor of *The People,* he guided the Socialist Labor party toward the implementation of his views. Based on his belief in political action as a form of revolutionary propaganda, he kept the S.L.P. alive. However, he gradually moved it away from its occasional penchant for running candidates for office, and after 1900 he deleted from the party platform the plank on ameliorative demands. At the same time, he dropped from membership rolls those middle-class moderates who favored reform measures. Also excluded were those who questioned the party discipline upon which he insisted.[13]

DeLeon's primary energies were expended on the labor movement, as he sought concrete means to reconstruct it into a class-conscious all-inclusive movement of wage earners. His failure to capture control of organized labor, specifically the dying Knights of Labor, in which he was active for several years, led him to resolve upon dual unionism, a course of action unpalatable to Marx, and one which has turned organized labor against a long list of radicals. At the end of 1895 he was expelled from the Knights for his untiring efforts to bend the Order to his views, after an illusory victory in which he had helped others deny Terence V. Powderly his perennial position of Grand Master Workman.

DeLeon proceeded to establish his own labor federation organized on an industry-wide basis and affiliated with the S.L.P. The Socialist Trade and Labor Alliance, never anything but DeLeon's tool, sought to undercut the A.F. of L. and the disappearing Knights. It served as a labor organization opposed both to capitalism and to the "faker" union leaders of the older federations. The Socialist Trade and Labor Alliance was endorsed by the S.L.P. despite the objections of some unionist members of the party who were committed personally to the strategy of "boring from within." The S.T. and L.A. was most active in areas where the A.F. of L. was weak, but it succeeded neither in organizing the unorganized nor in disrupting the A.F. of L. By 1898 the S.T. and L.A. was shrinking, its membership peaking at about 30,000. DeLeon had succeeded only in intensifying organized labor's hostility to the socialist cause.[14]

His personal authoritarianism and his ideological dogmatism resulted in the fragmentation of his own party at the very time when he was seeking to disrupt the existing labor movement. A few years later, in 1905, he attended the founding convention of the Wobblies and merged the S.T. and L.A. with the new organization. There, too, he was a disruptive influence, though his somewhat altered views coincided with the I.W.W.'s emphasis on revolutionary industrial unionism over party activity. He was expelled in 1908 when the Wobblies rejected political action. Despite his acceptance of syndicalist elements, in his eyes the political path remained an important means of revolutionary preparation, and he never completely abandoned the ballot. The remaining six years of DeLeon's life saw him almost exclusively concerned with his editing and party responsibilities. His legacy is a miniscule, tightly organized socialist party that revolves around his memory and has continued to assert his ideological interpretations decades after his death.

With DeLeon ends the thoroughly foreign stage of Marxism in the United States. The socialist movement that evolved as a counterthrust to DeLeon represented an American phase that succeeded in building a membership of predominantly native-born and in attaining influence across the nation. DeLeon had sought to relate Marxism to the American environment, for he believed that the United States would soon be ripe for revolution as a result of its rapid industrial development and sophistication. However, he was unable to attract natives to his programs, a fact reflective of his ideological bent and his personality. His emphasis on party discipline over individualism and class hostility over social solidarity were counter to American traditions.

Had the presentation of those ideas been less harsh or more guarded, his programs might have had greater success. But his antipathy toward compromise and his penchant for the dictatorial, when added to his threatening policy of dual unionism, precluded chances of American workers following his leadership. By the end of the century, his contribution in energizing the socialist movement had terminated in a vacuum.[15]

Confusion prevailed in the late nineties as various factions abandoned the Socialist Labor party. German and Jewish groups in New York broke with DeLeon in 1897 and 1898. The nucleus of the party seemed to be splitting off as a dissident group. Headed by Morris Hillquit, it claimed the party name and newspaper. Meanwhile, in the midsection of the country, native and immigrant radicals organized the Social Democracy of America. This unwieldy organization encompassed a faction dedicated to a form of communitarianism, behind the leadership of Eugene V. Debs, fresh from his Woodstock jail conversion to socialism, and a political faction, led by Victor Berger of Milwaukee. Debs and Berger joined forces in 1898 in bolting the Social Democracy, and formed their own Social Democratic party. Unity with the Hillquit group, with whom significant ideological rapport existed, was consummated in 1901 with the founding of a new national party, the Socialist Party of America.[16]

The new party, heavily middle-class and American in its composition, meant that, as one historian observes, "The day of organizing a special English-speaking branch of the socialist movement in America was gone." Leadership roles, however, continued to be exercised by immigrants, attesting to the strength of those who had emerged from the parent organizations. Aside from the well-known Debs, whose aversion to administrative responsibilities and fratricidal conflict led him to eschew involvement in party functions, leadership passed into the hands of the Austrian-born Victor Berger and the Russian-born Morris Hillquit. These two men built and shaped the one socialist party to play a significant role in American politics.[17]

The ideological similarities which had permitted unity did not result in a cohesive party. While party leaders sought the same collectivist social order and avoided dual unionism in order to win labor support, the American socialists found themselves as riddled with deep doctrinal disagreement as other socialist parties. A left wing of orthodox Marxists confronted a revisionist faction which clustered around Berger. A center faction or swing group clung to Hillquit. The fact that the left lacked dynamic and consistent leaders and that the right and center tended to converge resulted in a revisionist and reformist Marxist political party.

The orthodox minority stressed the Marxist dialectic, arguing that existing tensions between opposing forces in society were heading toward sudden upheaval and social transformation. The increasing misery and impoverishment of the masses in the face of the growing wealth of American capitalism meant continuing crises. The American experience of industrial development immersed in frequent labor bloodbaths served to verify Marxist theory. Revolution seemed to them imminent.

Therefore, the orthodox Marxist faction held that the party must offer the American masses propaganda and enlightenment, and encourage class consciousness. It must prevent the masses from following illusory reforms or gradualist change. The party itself must not offer mild curatives which might divert worker interest in the class struggle and revolutionary change. Rather, the party must prepare for direct action at the inevitable, cataclysmic moment when capitalism would collapse from its internal contradictions and be replaced by the collective ownership of the means of production.

The right wing of the Socialist party argued that socialism could be achieved gradually, possibly without violence. History had proved Marx erroneous in some of his predictions. Therefore his theories must be revised. The rightists questioned that social evolution was impoverishing the working class further and depressing the middle class to a propertyless status. They reasoned that the masses were less impoverished than in the earlier stage of capitalist development and, as a result, social tensions were decreasing. A revised strategy to achieve collective ownership was thus necessary. Rather than revolution, reformism, based on the utilization of the ballot was the appropriate tactic.

The right stressed immediate demands and the gradual, step-at-a-time nature of the class struggle. The aim of the party should be to capture a secure place in the structure of American society. Instead of confining itself to propaganda, the party must win the firm support not only of workers but also of farmers and even of the middle class. Once such support was obtained, the party could function as a legislative pressure group or win public office. Then reforms could be sought which would benefit the masses and encourage measures leading toward the long-range goal of collective ownership. Evolution was thus substituted for the dialectic as the emphasis was on immediate goals and contemporary conditions.

The center, moving toward the right in the party's early years, came to believe in political campaigns for the sake of victory rather than for their propaganda value. Accordingly, it endorsed appeals to the middle class, argued against antagonizing the American Federation of Labor, and even minimized collectivist planks in campaign platforms. For all practical purposes, the center became indistinguishable from the right.

At the Unity Convention of 1901, the orthodox faction was in the minority and a platform upholding immediate demands was passed. The gradualist ethos of the party never altered. To the chagrin of the left, the Socialist party resolved to support the organized labor movement, despite its pure-and-simple conservatism. Further, on an issue never wholly resolved, the party sought the allegiance of the farmer whose inherent radicalism rather than his status as a property owner was stressed. In the political sphere, the party campaigned avidly in municipal, state, and national elections, stressing the capture of offices instead of the agitational and propaganda value of the exercise. The grumbling of the left remained relatively ineffectual.[18]

In the limelight on the right was Victor Berger, a fixture on the National Executive Committee of the party, a perennial socialist candidate for municipal and Congressional offices, and the unchallenged leader of the most successful socialist movement in any American city. Berger (1860-1929) was born in the Austrian Empire to a middle-class Jewish family. He was educated at the Universities of Vienna and Budapest and, after two years of formal studies, as a result of a reversal in the family's economic status, emigrated in 1878. Berger settled in the city of Milwaukee, a not surprising choice. He immersed himself in the Germanic cultural life of the city. As a teacher and then an editor, he became caught up in the Turner movement, local fraternal societies around which German community life centered. Through his contact with workers, he cast aside his conservative and religious family traditions and committed himself to the nascent socialist organization in Milwaukee. For a brief time he belonged to the local branch of the S.L.P., but resigned over its tight centralization. By the end of the nineties, he was involved in radical politics nationally. He controlled the Milwaukee branch of the Socialist party and, in concert with the heavily German organized labor movement, within a few years led the party to local electoral victories.[19]

Berger saw his task as the rewriting of Marxist theory in order to relate it to American conditions. While he has sometimes been called an American Eduard Bernstein—the major German revisionist of Marxist doctrine—Berger's path was uniquely pragmatic. He clung to unamended Marxism where possible but where necessary, supported modifications beyond Bernstein's revisionism. His reading of theory and of the American environment convinced him that the coming of the collectivist society would be gradual but inevitable. Not until the end of his career did he agree with those revisionists who argued that the struggle itself had greater reality than long-range and possibly uncertain goals. The trend toward monopolistic production in the United States was in itself altering the nature of capitalism, Berger believed. He wished to promote the further development of monopolies and trusts into every industrial area able to accommodate large-scale production and distribution so that when that point was reached, private monopoly would be transformed via nationalization into public monopoly.[20]

According to his theories, neither force nor violence was required. Channels for legal change and the existence of universal manhood suffrage made bloodshed unnecessary. Moreover, he held, violently imposed systems could never take root. An enlightened public was as crucial as the development of monopolistic conditions. Therefore, Berger proposed that the party constantly agitate and educate in order to hasten the propitious moment. In his various electoral capacities he encouraged beneficial reforms which would ease the harshness of workers' lives and teach them to trust the socialists. It was necessary for the movement, he argued, that socialists refrain from the obstructionism in office which some Marxists advocated and, instead, assume responsibility and promote positive policies. The existing political process should be exploited for the duration.[21]

Based on these views, Berger supported the organized labor movement, retreating from an early policy of "boring from within" the A.F. of L. He came to regard the union as an exercise in worker solidarity, valid in its own right, and he ceased attempts to capture it. In a similar vein, he was willing to cooperate with nonsocialist reforming elements in the pursuit of social legislation of mutual interest. Flaunting party condemnation, he dared to chance collaboration with reformers, secure in his belief that his principles of nationalization and the class struggle were not threatened.

Berger refrained from describing the new order beyond the broadest lines of collectivism and democracy. His greatest concern was for the means of its initiation. Anxious as he was to eschew force at the baptism of the new society, he insisted that he would compensate expropriated property owners. Moreover, he explicitly disavowed a dictatorship in the name of the workers: the enlightened masses would build the new system. Thus, having predicted the inevitable transformation on the basis of evolving economic forces and public enlightenment, he believed that democratic collectivism would flower spontaneously.[22]

Berger's bookishness and heavy-handed rhetoric endowed him with the image of a Viennese professor. On the other hand, his bombastic personality coupled with his smooth, but firm, control of the Milwaukee socialists, gave him a lifetime reputation as a political boss. The peak of his career came in 1910 when he was elected in April to the Milwaukee Common Council at the same time that one of his protégés became mayor of the city; six months later Berger was elected to the House of Representatives as the first socialist Congressman.[23]

Berger's work in Congress has been described by one writer as "making Marx respectable." His knowledgeability, courtesy, and basic decorum could not help but modify the popular stereotype of the radical as bomb thrower. The presentation of socialist ideas within Congress mitigated against consideration of the movement as alien, threatening, or insignificant. Berger and the nonorthodox wing of the party maintained that his term in Congress verified their faith in the educational value of elective office. While in the House his efforts included social measures, such as old-age pensions and public welfare projects, constitutional amendments to foster direct democracy, and bills to nationalize the railroads. None was translated into law but their introduction in Congress served his purpose of exposing the American public to socialist views.[24]

The Socialist party flourished in the first dozen years of the twentieth century. In the background of its winning congressional representation was significant growth in membership, newspaper subscriptions, and votes at the ballot box. Membership grew from perhaps ten thousand at the party's founding to a peak of over one hundred thousand in 1912. By that date, the party was electing officials to state and municipal offices across the country, including the mayor's office in Schenectady, Butte, Berkeley, as well as in Milwaukee. In its national campaigns, its traditional candidate, Debs, amassed almost six percent of the votes cast in 1912. With reformist domination of party machinery unthreatened, a number of subsidiary educational institutions were founded and socialist clubs (the Intercollegiate Socialist Society) appeared on campuses throughout the nation. Socialism seemed to be making solid inroads among Americans.[25]

In the East, the acknowledged party leader was the urbane and sophisticated Morris Hillquit (1869-1933), who went from the S.L.P. to the reformist wing of the Socialist party. In addition to his party activism, he was renowned in New York City as a labor lawyer and public servant. Hillquit was born of Jewish parents in Riga in the Russian Empire. The son of a teacher, he was trained for the law after the family emigrated to the United States in 1885. While a student he worked in the needle trades and, years later he served as one of the chief advisers to the I.L.G.W.U. Hillquit entered the socialist movement from the Lower East Side Jewish ghetto, joining the Socialist Labor party. He came into conflict with the authoritarian DeLeon and, riding on the crest of his own popularity in the party, Hillquit led the walkout which irrevocably split the S.L.P. Hillquit, like Berger, had chafed under iron rule in a party theoretically devoted to equality.[26]

Hillquit was the main theorist of the Socialist party. Invariably, he was chosen to draw up major resolutions and policy statements, due in the main to his conciliatory approach rather than to any creative bent for the theoretical. Thus, he penned the controversial party planks on immigration and articulated the opposition to American participation in World War I. But he did not contribute significantly to socialist theory. Hillquit's contributions to the movement lay in two other areas: while reinforcing the emphasis of the right on evolutionary socialism, he brought to the party his considerable legal talents and he bent his energies to tying the dynamic Jewish labor movement of New York to the socialist cause.

Hillquit stressed the electoral path to socialist victory, arguing that the political struggle was more important than the economic struggle, and that, in fact, the ultimate aim of the labor movement was political: the capture of power through the ballot by the workers. From that vantage point Hillquit gave priority to welding a unified labor movement with the Socialist party. The fate of the movement, he wrote unequivocally, depended on securing unwavering labor support. "I have at all times maintained that the prime object of the Socialist Party is to organize the working class."[27]

To accomplish this aim, he served as the party's main combatant in well-publicized debates with leaders of both conservative and revolutionary labor. He challenged Samuel Gompers before the United States Commission on Industrial Relations and confronted Big Bill Haywood of the Wobblies at Cooper Union in New York before a large audience. To Gompers, Hillquit stressed the need for all labor unions to cooperate with the Socialist party for the sake of their mutual goals, and he argued with Haywood that sabotage and violence, and even the general strike, must be avoided in favor of political action by labor. Above all, he vetoed the dual unionist policy that had been forced on him in his early years, and pleaded for a unified effort.[28]

Hillquit's avoidance of revolutionary postures led him to take positions that sometimes echoed the reformism of nonsocialists. In his various campaigns for Congress from the Lower East Side, he and his coworkers whittled down their Marxist planks until the stress was on such measures as tenement safety regulations and legal protection for pushcart peddlers. His most successful, albeit losing, campaign for office was his race for mayor of New York City in 1917, where he polled a greater percentage of the votes than any socialist had before, and came in third in a field of four. But the leading issue in his campaign was his antiwar position rather than socialism.[29]

While his campaign and individual speeches reverberated in unrevolutionary tones, his fundamental commitment was that of a Marxist straining toward orthodoxy. As he came to accept many of Berger's positions, he, too, retained a belief in the class struggle, if only by ballot, and the disappearance of capitalism if the cooperation of the proletariat and the middle class

could be secured. His tendency to reconcile contradictory positions and factions blurred his image, but a biographer correctly
calls him the Marxist synthesizer of the labor and socialist
movements.[30]

The First World War shattered the Socialist party, and effectively destroyed the life work of its leaders. The fact of world
war was followed by the dismaying news that most European
socialists supported their nations at war, despite the movement's
commitment to peace and international brotherhood. In the
United States, the socialists used their propaganda organs to
support American neutrality, despite the protests and resignations
of members who believed that policy to be cloaking support
for the Central Powers. In 1917, at the American entry into the
war, the Socialist party held an emergency convention where
it announced its allegiance to the principles of internationalism
and working-class solidarity and declared its opposition to a
capitalist world war. Such a policy of dissent in the face of a
national war effort brought support from pacifists and other
wartime skeptics and persecution by the government.[31]

Various socialist newspapers lost their second-class mailing
privileges, including Berger's daily, the Milwaukee *Leader*, and
the New York *Call*, which served informally as Hillquit's
mouthpiece. In addition, many national and local party leaders
were prosecuted for violation of the Espionage Act through
their antiwar statements. A national hysteria gradually took
over press and public so that any form of dissent was called
disloyalty. At the end of the war the New York State Assembly
refused to seat five socialists and the United States Congress
twice excluded Victor Berger from the seat to which he had
legally been elected by the Fifth Congressional District of
Wisconsin.[32]

While such official pressures were brought to bear on the
reformist socialist leaders, an internal upheaval occurred within
the party. The orthodox Marxist wing experienced a renaissance
during the war. It attacked the reformist leaders, numerically
weaker due to wartime defections, for their failure to pursue

the antiwar policy vigorously enough The Bolshevik Revolution further energized the revolutionary left which now strenuously deprecated the party policy of immediate reforms and gradualist tactics within the capitalist structure. Leftists insisted on direct action preparatory to a revolutionary seizure of power.

Support for these revolutionary policies came from the mushrooming foreign-language federations of the party. Prior to the war these semi-autonomous federations had contained twenty-five or thirty percent of the party membership, but after the Russian Revolution their numbers expanded significantly so that in 1919 they made up fifty-three percent of the party. Slav immigrants who had never been aligned to the Socialist party rushed to sign their names on its membership rolls to symbolize their support for the new Russian government. These Russians, Lithuanians, Ukrainians, and other Slavs demonstrated little interest in American conditions, and their Eastern European outlook led them to support the most revolutionary rhetoric and leadership. The Socialist party, its leaders fearful of losing all contact with the American public, once again became an alien organization.[33]

Under such conditions, a new leadership displaced the old, and those party leaders who had known some success in relating their ideology to the American environment were challenged by those who wished to utilize foreign tactics and experience. The leader of the new wave was Louis C. Fraina (1892-1953), a self-educated young immigrant who years later, following his disillusionment with the Communist party, wrote that he had misunderstood the United States and taken for granted the freedoms of a liberal democracy. In 1918-19, however, he was certain that a direct actionist, highly disciplined revolutionary party in imitation of the Russian example could create a proletarian revolution against capitalism.[34]

Fraina had been brought from Italy to the United States as a three-year-old child, and grew up in the slums of New York City. His impoverished childhood led him to immerse himself in the literature of social protest. Upon interruption of his formal education at the age of thirteen, he worked as a clerk but soon was able to embark upon a journalistic career. He entered the radical movement and, finding factionalization endemic and theory often sidetracked by the "practical," by the age of twenty he had ". . . gone through three movements, the Socialist party, the I.W.W., and the Socialist Labor party.[35]

Before the war, Fraina was contemptuous of right-wing party leaders for what he saw as their abandonment of Marxism. But he himself did not challenge them explicitly to assume revolutionary postures. However, by war's end, as the leader of the Left Wing Section that would soon split off from the party, he cheered the Bolshevik seizure of power in the Russian Empire and dreamed of an American revolution, writing that everywhere "Capitalism is verging on collapse. . . ." Fraina denounced the leadership of the Socialist party as counterrevolutionary and he demanded that it accept new tactics. Instead of middle-class reforms and "parliamentary opportunism," the Socialist party must lead the American workers into the revolution itself.

The Socialist party, he argued, must be a revolutionary party in the Russian image. Electoral activity must be subsidiary, utilized only as propaganda, while economic organization should be stressed for its fostering of solidarity. The revolutionary party must immediately educate the workers for the forcible overthrow of capitalism, and for the establishment of a socialist system via a dictatorship of the proletariat. As a nascent communist, the future first International Secretary of the American Communist party demanded an unequivocal endorsement of the Leninist government in Russia. The reluctance of the older leadership of the Socialist party to embrace the new Russian government and its tactics convinced Fraina that another vehicle must be found through which to achive the socialist revolution in the United States.[36]

In early 1919, the left formed a rival institutional group within the party. The old leadership, attempting to retaliate, expelled several party branches, including a number of foreign-language federations, over a disputed election. The counter-thrusts ended in August, 1919, with a party schism. Thereafter, three separate parties existed all resting on socialist ideals, the Communist party, the Communist Labor party, and the old Socialist party. The first two lived virtually an underground existence, while the last sought to continue on traditional paths, though weakened, shrunken, and uninfluential. The Socialist party, consisting now of only 26,000 members, followed its former leaders, Berger and Hillquit, and again nominated Debs for the Presidency, but its potential had disappeared in the midst of war and schism.[37]

The Anarchists

Anarchism was an international movement in the eighties and nineties. It grew in the soil of economic and social unheaval characteristic of the Western nations during the nineteenth century. Anarchism offered a comprehensive and searing critique of industrial society, and spelled out its own panacea. More fundamental in its criticism than lucid in its ideology, the movement attracted a scattered following throughout Europe, especially in the Latin countries, and in the United States.

Anarchists denounced the nineteenth-century liberal state as energetically as they rejected feudalism and absolutism. They attacked the principle of representation, as well as the very notion of government. The bourgeois social order, resting upon the foundation of the liberal state, was dismissed along with the capitalistic free enterprise system from which it sprang. Political reforms and welfare legislation were considered innocuous measures which served only to assure the misguided in their acceptance of prevailing values and institutions.[38]

The thrust of the anarchists' attack was upon the inability of Western liberalism to satisfy individual needs. In their eyes, after a century of constitutional and economic reform, the centralized, industrialized state regimented the masses and denied their humanity. Greater power and efficiency in the hands of the state, they held, would fail to alleviate injustice; the whole structure must be pulled down abruptly and a new society created.

Anarchism as a social theory was based upon opposition to all forms of coercive authority; conversely, noncoercive association and cooperation were upheld. Mutual cooperation among small groups, the natural form of association for mankind, would be attainable once private property, with its inherent divisive tendencies, was abolished. Individual groups would produce and consume cooperatively, and these decentralized units would join in a free federation for the purpose of common action. Such collective economic activities within a framework of decentralization represented the essence of anarchism. It was rooted in socialism, the ideology from which it emerged, but anarchism departed from that school of thought in its rejection of the state. Whereas Marx was content with the gradual withering away of the state, anarchists demanded its complete disappearance at the moment of the revolution.[39]

The revolution was to erupt at the instant when conspirators had undermined the old order. Thereafter, the emancipated people themselves would undertake the formation of their decentralized cooperative society. Neither dialectical force nor a dictatorship of the proletariat was required. Insurrection, following earlier acts of terror or direct action—the propaganda of the deed—valued for symbolic and educational purposes, would inaugurate the new order.[40]

The technique of propaganda by the deed had a frightening impact on the public mind. Prominent personalities everywhere were subject to physical attack by anarchists, who believed in the apocalyptic value of revolutionary terrorism, and by the criminal and the deranged whom public opinion indiscriminately labeled anarchists. At a time when a semblance of class warfare pervaded the Western world, assassinations became commonplace: a president of France, an empress of Austria, a king of Italy, a prime minister of Spain, and a president of the United States. All of these murders were attributed to the international anarchist movement, and the deed overshadowed the word.[41]

In the United States anarchist ideas, introduced by immigrants, played an influential role in some labor circles in the eighties. The pioneers, heroes, and martyrs of the anarchist movement in this country were those individuals involved in the Haymarket Affair in Chicago at the height of the eight-hour campaign. The holocaust of the Haymarket caused a fundamental reshaping of the advocacy by the immigrant anarchists of propaganda by the deed.

Chicago was the focus of the agitation for the eight-hour day. It was also a heavily foreign population center, nearly fifty percent of its inhabitants being immigrants. Its large German colony was permeated with socialist and anarchist doctrines, as yet not wholly distinct from each other. Up until 1883, social revolutionaries of various stripes, many of whom had fled from legislation which Bismarck had instituted to undermine German radicalism, belonged to the same groups. In that year, however, a national congress was held under the sponsorship of two Chicago labor leaders, August Spies and Albert R. Parsons. At the Congress, a branch of the anarchist International Working People's Association (the Black International) was formed, and it officially separated the movement into an anarchist and a socialist division. The Chicago anarchists, working through the trade-union movement, played a central role in labor's development for the next three years.[42]

These anarchists wished to encourage the development of class-conscious trade unions which would eventually serve as the basic units of the new order. Violence was upheld as a legitimate tool of the workers, and insurrection was the means through which the existing system would be destroyed. Believing that only force could pave the way for the disappearance of private property and the coming of the era of cooperative federation, they denigrated political action. Dynamite, explosives, and assassination were advocated. Based on this ideology, the Chicago anarchist movement grew to perhaps

7,000 members, attracting Germans and Bohemians to their organizations and newspapers. Native response was slight, and only one of their handful of publications appeared in the English language.[43]

The anarchists unenthusiastically supported the eight-hour movement in Chicago. At first they had dismissed the campaign as a compromise with the wage system and a self-deceptive cure-all fostered by the Federation of Organized Trades, the forerunner of the A.F. of L. However, recognizing that the campaign was becoming a national manifestation of labor solidarity, they served as leaders in the city whose labor force most vigorously responded to the call for a national strike on May 1, 1886. The anarchists rejoiced in the fact that the atmosphere was as tense as in 1877, the year of major labor upheavals nationally, and they announced that the country had entered a prerevolutionary period.[44]

Eighty thousand workers struck throughout the city of Chicago. In the midst of the strike, police fired into a crowd of strikers and scabs at the McCormick Harvester Company, resulting in the deaths of four workers. The anarchists at once called a protest meeting for the next evening, May 4, at Haymarket Square. While tension filled the atmosphere and extra police surrounded the area, an audience of several thousand people listened quietly to angry addresses by the anarchists. For reasons still unknown, the police chose to disperse the crowd shortly before the meeting's scheduled closing, and in the resulting confusion, a bomb exploded, killing one policeman and wounding several others. The subsequent melee led to the deaths of seven policemen and the wounding of many bystanders. Eight leaders of the Chicago anarchist movement were arrested, despite lack of direct evidence of complicity. They were convicted " . . . after a trial which cast considerable doubt on the character and processes of American justice." Ultimately, four of the men were hanged, one committed suicide in the county jail. Seven years later when this earliest of "red scares" had somewhat abated, the three survivors were pardoned by Governor Altgeld. Seven of the eight men were German-speaking and their ordeal made an enormous impact on immigrant revolutionaries of various persuasions.[45]

August Spies (1855-1887) and Albert R. Parsons (1848-1887) were the most prominent of the Chicago anarchists, with Spies dominant among the German-speaking members and Parsons, a native American, the most influential in the smaller English-speaking anarchist faction. Spies had come to the United States from agrarian Central Germany when he was seventeen years of age. As the son of a forester, he had not been exposed to industrial conditions and consequently he was appalled at the exploitation of the workers which he witnessed in the United States. After a few years at varied jobs, Spies became a socialist activist in 1877. Attracted to the unfamiliar ideology, he soon mastered Marx and other European economists. But he quickly moved toward an anarchist emphasis, as the events of 1877 convinced him that ". . . the brute force with which the . . . wage-slaves were met on all sides impressed upon me the necessity of the like."

Spies joined the *Lehr und Wehr Verein,* an armed club of German radicals whose purposes were twofold: to provide protection from potential state militia action and to impress upon workingmen the possibility of meeting force with force. He also ran for public office on the Socialist ticket, promoting such political action solely for propagandistic purposes, for he was by then convinced that ". . . the economic emancipation . . . can be achieved through an economic struggle only. . . ." Most of his time was spent as an organizer for the anarchist movement and, after 1880, as an editor of German-language anarchist sheets.[46]

At the trial resulting from the violence at Haymarket, Spies and the others delivered lengthy addresses prior to the pronouncement of their sentences. He summarized his philosophical views as he addressed the court ". . . as the representative of one class to the representative of another." He explained that the wage system was the cause of existing social inequities. He predicted the imminence of violent revolution, in which the downtrodden masses would rise and expropriate the possessing classes. A new system of common ownership and universal cooperation, in essence, anarchism, would initiate an era of brotherhood.

Spies's more dramatic oration was saved for the hangman: "There will come a time when our silence in the grave will be more powerful than the voices you strangle today."[47]

The martyrdom of the Haymarket eight scarred the various revolutionary movements in the United States as decisively as the Paris Commune of 1871 marked European politics for the next several decades. In the latter instance, European radicals learned that the modern state did not collapse when confronted with barricaded streets. Centralized and industrialized states possessed both the power and the will to suppress urban insurrection; this was one factor in the acceptance by hitherto underground movements of newly available legal political and economic channels of dissent, such as suffrage and unionization. In the United States, the powerful effect of Haymarket was recognizable in the less strident tones of anarchist orators.

Immediately following the executions, the anarchists retreated from their advocacy of propaganda by the deed and minimized the emphasis on force. No longer did their newspapers print recipes for the manufacture of dynamite. The earlier muted reminders to readers that force ought not be used against individuals became a commonplace in anarchist speeches. At the same time, socialists took great pains to clarify the wide divergences between their ideology and anarchist doctrines. The two movements would henceforth follow paths that seldom crossed.[48]

The personality which dominated the New York faction of the anarchist movement and brought some measures of cohesiveness to the various groups across the eastern half of the country was Johann Most (1846-1906). It was Most who had really paved the way for the holding of the national congress at Pittsburgh in 1883, a year after his immigration to the United States from London. And it was also Johann Most who bore great responsibility for the image of violence that stamped anarchism in the United States, even though he himself never was involved in a violent act.

The propaganda by the deed which had resulted in the tragedy of the Haymarket Affair was reflected in Most's life as farce. Everywhere he went, he was jailed for the vitriolic articles he published and the furious speeches he delivered. His life was marked by imprisonment following every major incident in which anarchism was believed to be involved; he lived the deed through the word. He was sentenced in England to sixteen months in prison as a result of his endorsement of the assassination of Tsar Alexander II of Russia, he served a year in jail in New York for his remarks following the Haymarket executions, and he was indirectly implicated in the assassination of President William McKinley and imprisoned for one year: Most had the ill fortune to have published an article by Karl Heinzen on murder as a revolutionary weapon on the very day that McKinley was shot.

Most's aggressive temperament, reminiscent, in fact, of the violently authoritarian streak in Heinzen, led him to support individual acts of terrorism as an instrument in the class struggle. His newspaper, *Freiheit,* published information on the proper handling of bombs and advice on the home manufacture of nitroglycerine, which other anarchist sheets republished. After 1886, Most disavowed terroristic activities, and specifically condemned the assassination attempt on the life of Henry Clay Frick during the strike at Homestead by Alexander Berkman, a young Russian anarchist. But Most's propaganda had been so shrill that for the remaining twenty years of his life he was plagued by his earlier encouragement of insurrectionary methods.[49]

Most was born in Augsburg, Germany, in 1846, and by the

age of twenty-four he was a fiery socialist serving his first prison term for revolutionary propaganda. In the seventies he began to edit radical newspapers, endured three jail terms for his writings, and was twice elected to the Reichstag as a Social Democrat. He lived in England from 1878 to 1882, where he began the publication of his weekly, *Freiheit*, which would occupy him for the rest of his life. While in England, he became a convert to Bakuninist anarchist theories, for which he was expelled from the German Social Democratic party.[50]

Johann Most brought with him to the United States the ideas of the Russian anarchist Michael Bakunin, whose romanticized insurrectionism gave him a distinctive role in the revolutionary movements of the century. Like Bakunin, Most's aim was to organize society spontaneously from the bottom up rather than to organize society coercively from the top down. No governmental machinery would be utilized. Most carefully drew a line between his position and that of revolutionaries who wished to establish a communist or a so-called "people's state," and he attacked such notions as self-contradictory hybrids.[51]

Most, like his mentor, Bakunin, became enraged when discussing the institutions which he considered to be the greatest exploiters of the masses—private property and organized religion —both of which perpetuated the existence of the state. In his most famous pamphlet, "The Beast of Property," Most argued that the United States was more blatantly under the rule of money and monopoly than any other nation. Therefore the American historical mission was to demonstrate dramatically the helplessness of the masses before the "beast of prey" and the necessity of a war of extermination. Churches, which glorified the poverty of the masses, must be swept aside along with capitalists and bureaucrats in the whirlwind of the revolution. [52]

Most had no patience with piecemeal programs, such as the eight-hour movement that the Chicago anarchists had supported. Even unionization of the workers had no attraction for him.

He preferred simply to await the uprising of the masses whose ripeness for revolution appeared manifest to him as a result of the crises of overdeveloped capitalism. The moment seemed to him to be so imminent that he believed that only an example was needed. He often said, "If I had one hundred decided men at my disposal, then I would call for a revolution in New York tomorrow.[53]

In his last years, Most moved away from this mystique of violence. He minimized what his biographer, Rudolf Rocker, called a sentimental interpretation of the coming of the revolution, and he supported the anarcho-syndicalism that appeared in European labor circles. But in the main, and despite his rejection of individual terroristic acts, Most's career revolved about his belief in the possibility of the destruction of the state, the creative act which would permit the emergence of the cooperative federated order. He remained contemptuous of the Marxist strategy of seizing and manipulating the apparatus of the state. While Most, unlike Bakunin, did come to recognize that urban insurrection was unrealistic, he never appreciated the power and invincibility of the state, one of the central facts of the nineteenth century.[54]

After the death of Johann Most in 1906, the anarchist groups in America were dominated by two personalities whose careers were molded at least partially by their reactions to Most's influence. Both were Jewish immigrants from Tsarist Russia who settled in the United States in the eighties at a time when Most's stress on the deed pervaded the anarchist movement. Emma Goldman (1869-1940) and Alexander Berkman (1870-1936) embodied the spirit of alienated intellectual revolutionaries whose sensitivity to injustice convinced them that immediate direct action was the only justifiable policy. Emma Goldman's revolutionary ideals began to crystallize in the trauma of the Haymarket hangings, the same year that she and her sister had arrived, impoverished, in the land of promise. Berkman, as an eleven-year-old schoolboy in St. Petersburg, was captivated by the drama of the revolutionaries whose assassination of Alexander II reverberated in his classroom. Both young people quickly gravitated to Russian-speaking radical groups in New York City, and in 1889 they consummated a personal relationship whose professional aspects lasted for almost fifty years.[55]

Their baptism into revolutionary activism occurred in the midst of the Homestead strike of 1892. Viewing the situation through the prism of the rigid class lines of Russia, both misinterpreted Homestead. Goldman and Berkman were stunned by the news of Pinkertons descending upon steelworkers, and their own outrage convinced them that the moment was ripe for revolution. Berkman carried through an unsuccessful attempt to assassinate Henry Clay Frick, an associate of Carnegie, in the belief that an *attentat* would ignite the fuse. Workers would rise and destroy the capitalist system. But the results were an unimpressed working class, fourteen years of imprisonment for Berkman, and realization by both young revolutionaries that their tactics had been misguided.[56]

Their subsequent abandonment of propaganda by the deed spelled its demise in the anarchist movement in the United States. The press and public continued to see the hand of anarchism behind violent events, including the assassination of McKinley by the confused Leon Czolgosz, and in 1903 enthusiastically approved the first legislation to restrict immigration on the basis of opinion: an acknowledged anarchist could no longer emigrate to the United States. But Emma Goldman, safely within the confines of the country—or so it seemed—continued anarchist agitational campaigns unabated through the word. In later years, she denied that she had ever approved of individual violence. When pressed, she would sidestep the issue and argue that the violence of the organized state far outweighed any forceful acts committed by those anarchists who were compelled to the deed by consciences outraged over institutional exploitation.[57]

Emma Goldman and Alexander Berkman, through the pages of *Mother Earth*, a journal which the two edited alternately over a dozen years, sought to bring the message of anarchism to the public. Both of them believed in the need to reach English-speaking Americans, and they scolded fellow propagandists whose narrow agitational horizons included only immigrant communities. Goldman undertook annual cross-country tours and was able to attract crowds of both the committed and the curious. These thrusts into the heartland of the United States represented the movement's first agitational success among native Americans since Albert Parsons had built his small Chicago circle of anarchists in the eighties. But the Goldman tours twenty years later occurred when the strains and tensions affecting the workers were beginning to be cushioned by Progressive Era reforms. Moreover, organized labor's basic support for the existing framework served to lock labor into a conservative, nonmilitant stance. Thus, worker discontent was channeled into politically and economically acceptable areas of the American system, and the chance of anarchist revolutionaries building a national following were slimmer than they had ever been.[58]

Emma Goldman was a victim of the ugly notoriety that had been heaped on Frances Wright in an earlier day. Like the aristocratic Anglo-Saxon reformer of the Jacksonian Era, the Russian-born Jewish revolutionary was attacked and derided as a dangerous moral and political influence. However illusory her threat to the American system, her sponsorship of social revolution and her challenge to traditional values brought upon her, as a woman, the most malicious newspaper attacks aimed at any contemporary radical.

Her advocacy of social revolution did not obscure her commitment to immediate improvement in living and working conditions, one of the reasons for her break with Most. Moreover, again like Frances Wright, Emma Goldman focused upon the role of women in America. She crusaded for female emancipation as an inherent part of the general struggle for freedom, and did not hesitate to attack the narrow middle-class female suffrage movement. Full emancipation for women required economic equality, the availability of birth control information, and the abolition of the double standard. For these views as well as for her own sexual independence, she was vilified as a symbol of free love, the traditional charge pressed against a woman radical. But for Emma Goldman, every injustice had to be confronted. Her dedication to the anarchist movement was essentially the result of her humanitarianism. That, in essence, was her radicalism.

Alexander Berkman's revolutionary bent went hand in hand with a scholarly mind. His commitment to social revolution stemmed from his reading of Chernyshevsky and other contemporary Russian novelists whose works seemed to have endowed the impressionable boy with a need for a cause. His lifetime devotion to anarchist ideals, toughened and streamlined by his years of imprisonment as a young man, hardened his image. Personal contact with Berkman, however, always contradicted the external image, for he remained essentially a quiet, unassuming, even gentle individual whose sensitivity and compassion inspired warmth in others. Somewhat uneasy on the public platform and personally disoriented for a few years after his release from Western Penitentiary, Berkman nevertheless inspired trust in the crowds of immigrant workers whom he addressed. The purpose of the anarchist movement for Berkman was simply to encourage his listeners to greater self-awareness and social consciousness. Despite his basically intellectual commitment to the movement, the human being rather than doctrine was always uppermost in his mind.[59]

Goldman and Berkman emphasized to their readers the fraud and hypocrisy inherent in the republican system of government. They insisted that "no political system has ever equaled popular suffrage as an instrument of enslavement . . . the ballot box is the most potent factor for well-ordered oppression and exploitation. It hypnotizes its victims into the belief of political sovereignty. . . ." They pointed to the fundamental injustice of binding resolutions and majority decisions which inevitably meant that the individual lacked freedom. The American political process, as any other, manipulated its populace who, unlike victims of more clumsy systems, did not recognize their own subjugation.[60]

They argued against attempting to reform the political structure for, to them, under any guise, government was an unnecessary and coercive system which always sought to deny the individual the exercise of his free will. By their definition, no government was exempt from such a charge, and Goldman and Berkman could only scoff when they observed radicals of other persuasions pursue political reform. The Wobblies, for whom Emma Goldman especially had great respect and affection, seemed to her in their peripatetic pursuit of political goals totally confused. The Social Democrats, for whom the anarchists usually saved their greatest sarcasm, were to them not only misguided but deceitful and opportunistic in their political strategy.

The anarchists attacked what they, at their most generous, called the folly of parliamentary socialism. They believed that both European and American Marxists had fatally reversed the teachings of Marx on economics as the foundation of politics. His disciples erroneously sought to move the scene of the revolution from the factory to the parliaments and congresses. Such a strategy, dependent upon capturing votes and upholding constitutional legalities, ultimately would strengthen existing institutions. Those who support the proletariat, argued the anarchists, must never seek political reforms but, rather, stand in firm opposition. Such arguments by Goldman and Berkman often ended in outright dismissal of the American socialists as "conservative, retrograde, bigoted . . . wardheelers."[61]

The counterstrategy which Goldman and Berkman offered was that of direct action leading to eventual insurrection. The systematic assertion of the economic power of the workers meant organization, industrial sabotage, and the general strike. The general strike was seen as the most logical and effective instrument available to the workers. Capital, Goldman argued, was organized nationally and, thus, labor must organize as a class in order to confront management successfully. Cooperation by workers in all branches of an industry were the necessary steps toward a general strike which, in itself, bore the seeds of social revolution. Moreover, industrial unionism and worker unity would be the essential ingredients in the shaping of the system of production and distribution in the free society of the future. At the same time, anarchists insisted that revolutionary unionism and the general strike must be viewed as means to the end of social revolution. Insurrection and expropriation were unavoidable and necessary if a free order were to result.[62]

Emma Goldman was profoundly impressed with French syndicalism. After her meeting with syndicalist leaders at the Anarchist Congress in France in 1900, she sought to introduce their ideas to the American radical movement. Addressing herself to the most class-conscious American workers, she explained that syndicalism was the "economic expression of Anarchism." She described its major thrust as the education of the workers. Syndicalism taught them to repudiate the wage system and individual strikes, contracts, and negotiations. Its aim was the full liberation of the workers from oppressive institutions and the reconstruction of society into free federated groupings.[63]

The anarchists attempted to reach workers and everyone willing to listen. To limit their propaganda to the disinherited, they argued, would be a mistake. Members of the "respectable classes" often were susceptible to new ideas. Moreover, the future society would be classless, and therefore propaganda must be directed to all men and women, for all were to be liberated from authority. At times, Goldman and Berkman felt sanguine as to their success: the middle class was beginning to listen, attracted on ethical grounds, and interested in the strategy of passive resistance, while American workers were becoming convinced of the efficacy of revolutionary methods. But at other times it was hard not to see "... how little dent one makes with all one's effort." The years in the wilderness sometimes seemed endless.[64]

These two immigrant anarchists, like Johann Most before

them, built on ideas of European pioneers in the radical movement. For Goldman and Berkman, Peter Kropotkin, the Russian anarchist, was the seminal influence. From Kropotkin they developed their critiques of industrial society, buttressed by insights from American philosophical anarchists, especially Thoreau. Goldman and Berkman offered no more details about the future federated order than had their European mentor and, like most social seers, they argued that the new framework would itself supply dimensions that were unpredictable in advance. The crucial issue, which was the key to their critique of the existing system and their concern for the new, was the role of the individual. Society must offer unrestricted liberty to the individual, and thus the outline of the new order became that of a harmonious blending of individual and social instincts. As to whether human nature could cope with emancipation and its attendant responsibilities, the anarchists could only answer that the caged animal is never the same as the liberated animal. The liberation of human beings was expected to bring the release of the human spirit with its vast potentialities.[65]

The anarchist movement in the United States and the American phase of the careers of Emma Goldman and Alexander Berkman were shipwrecked in the upheaval of World War I and its aftermath. Goldman and Berkman, unlike many contemporary radicals, did not dilute their doctrines to support the war effort. They continued to favor internationalism, to oppose national wars, and to stress civil liberties. The exigencies of the crisis, however, forced them to minimize their anarchistic propaganda and to spend their energies on wartime issues: preparedness, conscription, freedom of the press, and the Mooney Case. The two organized the No-Conscription League which encouraged conscientious objectors to refuse induction into the army. They attacked the Espionage Act of June 15, 1917, and were promptly arrested and charged with conspiring against the draft. After conviction, they spent almost two years in federal penitentiaries, from which they attemtped to keep their publications alive and to encourage other dissenters to continue resistance to the wartime policies of the Wilson Administration.

Emma Goldman's career seemed in so many ways to revolve around the issue of civil liberties. She defended the civil rights of presidential assassin Leon Czolgosz, while all other radicals, including Berkman, turned away from him. She was outspoken in her support for the dissemination of birth control information when it tended to increase the already considerable opposition to her public lecturing. She never diminished her efforts to help all radical and minority groups whose freedoms of the press or of speech were threatened at any time.[66]

Berkman, who in 1916 had begun to publish *The Blast*, his own anarchist newspaper in San Francisco, was indicted for conspiracy in the Preparedness Parade Bomb Case of 1916 for which Tom Mooney, a labor organizer, and Warren Billings, an associate, were convicted. Apparently uninvolved with the incident, Berkman fought extradition proceedings from New York to California following his anti-conscription trial. Berkman and those around him interpreted the indictment as an effort to silence all radicals, but despite the pressures Berkman remained philosophical if not undaunted, and organized and propagandized while out on bail before serving his term.[67]

Upon their release at the end of 1919, Goldman and Berkman were expelled from the United States, with two hundred other assorted unfortunates caught in Attorney General Mitchell Palmer's raids. En route to Russia on the *S.S. Buford*, Berkman admitted to his diary, "It is hard to be torn out of the soil one has rooted in for over 30 years, and to leave the labors of a lifetime behind." But he looked forward to the work of social transformation in Russia. A few years later, after their disillusionment with the Russian regime and their self-imposed exile from the Motherland, Emma Goldman wrote for both of them that ". . . the political machine everywhere has proven itself utterly inadequate to solve great world problems. . . . What a mess political leaders have made, but [the] masses are also hopeless. & [sic] yet it is only they who can solve problems."[68]

That Goldman and Berkman should spend their last decades

in exile from two nations, wandering from country to country, was more poignant than surprising. In a world of increasing centralization and regimentation, these self-proclaimed anarchists stood unmoved as champions of decentralization and individualism. However blurred their visions might be, as a biographer has suggested, in distinguishing between governmental unresponsiveness and blatant repression, they clearly recognized the implicit threat of the modern centralized industrial state that liberals and other radicals could not acknowledge. They saw poverty in the midst of technical progress, and unlike others, they sensed the psychological dehumanization of the urban-industrial order. The tag of anarchism which they wore haunted them during their lifetimes and condemned them to the dust heap of history, but their ethical ideals and the acuteness of their vision after two generations ring clear.[69]

The influence of the immigrant radical proved to be fleeting, as World War I and its aftermath served to terminate abruptly the increasing public awareness of radical teachings. Radicalism was seen as a decided threat and, with immigrants and radicals linked in the eyes of the public, all immigrants became even more unwelcome. The American public endorsed a reversal of the traditional open-door policy on immigration, approving the Congressional restrictionist measures of 1921 and 1924. The National Origins Act, based on racial quotas favorable to northwestern Europeans, allowed no exceptions for possible political or religious exiles. No longer would radical immigrants enter the United States as refugees in search of a home.

Times had changed. The American public had lost some of the confidence of youth, and suspicion was more frequent than openness. The nation was stronger than ever, yet felt more vulnerable than it had in the long-ago days of Robert Dale Owen. Thus ended the saga of the radical immigrant.

CHAPTER VI

The Profile of the Radical Immigrant

THE MORE THAN TWO DOZEN IMMIGRANT RADICAL ACTIVISTS CON-
sidered here stoked the fires of social protest and criticism for
the century which began in 1820. Through their organizational
and propagandistic efforts they succeeded in introducing new
currents of thought to an American audience that sometimes
listened and reacted. As a group, these radical immigrant personalities posed a number of significant challenges to the liberal
democratic state and the free enterprise system as they developed
over the century.

The radical immigrants tended to be young men and women
who had received their education in the Old World prior to their
immigration. Consequently, most of them arrived with fixed
values and definite perspectives. Their youthfulness, characteristic of most immigrants, was reflected in a median age at immigration of twenty-six,[1] and often resulted in their assuming
major responsibility in various political and social movements
before middle age. George Henry Evans led the workingmen's
movement in New York at the age of twenty-four. The average
age of the German Forty-eighters who played major roles in
the nascent Republican party as spokesmen for their community
was only thirty; Ernestine Rose was thirty years old when she
led the successful fight for married women's property rights in
New York, and Alexander Berkman was merely twenty-two years
old when he undertook his *attentat* on the life of Henry Clay
Frick. In these instances and others, youthful responsibility was
due to two factors. In the first place, there was the enthusiasm
of youth coupled with unusual intellectual maturity, and sec-

ondly, there was no radical old guard to be shunted aside. The radical immigrants had an open theater in which to function.

Unlike most immigrants the majority of the radicals enjoyed middle-class backgrounds. Of the twenty-eight figures presented herein, only six were genuinely of the working class. They were: William Heighton, a cordwainer, George Henry Evans, a printer, Wilhelm Weitling, a tailor, Adolph Germer and Ed Boyce, miners, and Louis Fraina, a factory worker. At the other extreme, three of the radicals came from backgrounds of considerable wealth: Robert Dale Owen, son of the renowned Scottish manufacturer and philanthropist, Frances Wright, reared in the life style appropriate to the upper class in early nineteenth-century Scotland, and Mathilde Franziska Giesler-Anneke who grew to maturity amid the security of wealth and privilege in Westphalia. Most of these people, however, were children of civil servants, ministers, teachers, doctors, or of the lower-middle class.

The great majority of these radicals were products of the European educational systems ranging from private tutors for a few to university training for half of the group. The fact that roughly fifty percent of the radical immigrants were university educated is further indication of their uniqueness.

In a number of instances the radicals appear to have been influenced by parental liberalism. Liberal fathers, some of whom were outspoken in their support for revolutionary ideologies and movements, shaped the views of Robert Dale Owen, Frances Wright, George Henry Evans, Karl Heinzen, and Friedrich Sorge. Owen and Sorge came into contact with revolutionary currents through their fathers' sympathies, while Frances Wright as a young girl, romanticized memories of a father who died too early, leaving behind a library that was a testament to his support for the French Revolution. Evans accepted his father's support for English agrarianism, and Heinzen, who believed his father to be a royalist, knew that in the older Heinzen's youth he had supported republicanism. But the radicalism of the majority, as far as its origins can be traced, stemmed from reflective and sensitive minds as well as emotional temperaments, acting against the tumultuous nineteenth-century environment.

In a few cases these immigrants embraced a radical vision of society only after immigration. Autobiographical writings of August Spies, Emma Goldman, Victor Berger, and Morris Hillquit reveal that their interest in social problems was really awakened after their acquaintance with the urban-industrial civilization of the United States. Spies directly noted that in agrarian Germany he had lacked awareness of emergent industrial society, while Berger clearly was introduced to those conditions as a young schoolteacher in Milwaukee's Turner movement. But these individuals were a decided minority. By the time of their arrival on these shores most of them had been molded into confirmed militants by their European education, experiences, and horizons.

The religious upbringing and training of the radicals tended to have become cumbersome and unwanted intellectual baggage which was shrugged off at an early age. One-fourth of the radicals were of Jewish background and one-fourth of Roman Catholic education and training. The remainder were divided among various Protestant sects, especially Presbyterian and Lutheran. Those whose religious experience was authoritarian tended to be fierce in their secularist loyalties, sharing with all converts a tendency toward the fanatical. In every case, the Enlightenment and the rationalist tradition which evolved from it became the framework which substituted for a religious outlook.

As might be anticipated, a minority of the radicals were women. Perhaps as a direct result of the extra dimension involved in breaking through the cloistered walls of the nineteenth-century role assigned to woman, all four of these radicals were without exception fiercely independent and uncompromising spirits. Frances Wright, Ernestine Rose, and Emma Goldman were outspoken public lecturers in support of unpopular causes, while Madame Anneke promoted education for women despite the overwhelming disapproval of the German-American community. All of these women followed autonomous paths in their public careers which separated them from husbands or lovers, and braved annulments or divorces in the face of community disapproval. None flinched from condemnation but, rather, continued to pursue humanistic goals which feminists of a later century still seek to fulfill. The psychological and temperamental uniqueness of these women merits further exploration.

Very few of the radicals trod a path that led them to ideological conservatism. The classical odyssey from the far left to the far right, often the result of a psychological need to atone for an errant youth, was not characteristic of this group. Only Robert Dale Owen fell into this pattern, perhaps in order to rebel against his father, since young Owen, alone among the entire sample, built his radical career closely upon his father's teachings. However, while a psychological study might focus on Owen as an example of the generational theme of Fathers against Sons, here it can only be indicated that Owen became a thorough-going conservative in repudiation of all of his early beliefs. Friedrich Hassaurek and Friedrich Kapp severely tempered their views as they grew older. Thomas Brothers, too, ended as a conservative, but his flirtation with radicalism had been briefer and seemingly more superficial than that of the others. Aside from these four, three radicals drifted away from activist careers, Wilhelm Weitling, Ed Boyce, and Friedrich Sorge, but they did not reject their youthful ideologies. The vast majority spent their entire lives from the moment of radicalization until their final years as proponents of their various causes.

There were four different factors leading to the immigration of these radicals. Of those who came in childhood or adolescence, economic pressures had brought their families to the United States. Political persecution caused more than a third of the radicals to emigrate. Religious restrictions and persecution were background factors in the immigration of the Jewish radicals. Finally, a very small proportion of the sample emigrated in order to promote radical causes in the United States.

The motivation involved in the evolution of these radicals falls into three categories. Those who were workers themselves responded to the economic and social stimuli in their daily lives. A second group came to its radical orientation through feelings of guilt inspired by privileged positions. The largest group, those of the middle class, were politically or culturally alienated from their societies. Class itself amounts to a partial explanation of motive.

Craftsmen, such as Evans, Heighton, and Weitling knew the exacting conditions, long hours, dim lighting, and polluted air found in workshops throughout the country. They were familiar with the limited security of men whose crafts were being displaced and whose sole recourse was to seek work in other shops where conditions were likely to be very much the same. The miners, Ed Boyce and Adolph Germer, were personally aware of the dangers and diseases resulting from life underground for those who wielded pick and shovel. Without stable organization or protective legislation, the extent of worker dependence and helplessness was evident.

This entire group of radical immigrants understood through direct experience the lack of autonomy characteristic of workers' lives. The injustice of unending poverty and sacrifice to which the producers of the national wealth were subjected radicalized them. They demanded government action, whether it was the ten-hour day, mine safety legislation, or nationalization of major industries. Alternately, they led their fellow workers into direct economic action, whether through strikes, boycotts, or militant unionization, or they sought to create labor parties. The direct correlation between their experiences and their activism needs little documentation.

Among that small proportion accustomed to great wealth, privilege bred a sense of guilt and of responsibility to others. Frances Wright, for example, described the psychological jolt she experienced when she fully recognized the existence of poverty in the world. Madame Anneke, too, was affected by the disparity between her own position and that of the poor in her native Westphalia, and her emotional reaction was in part responsible for her involvement in radical circles in the 1840's.

By far the most profound sense of guilt was acknowledged by Robert Dale Owen. He was driven to bend his energies to building a more humane world where reason prevailed, and where the elite demonstrated a paternal interest in the lives of the masses.

Such a conscience-driven reformer is not unique in the annals of radical movements. These individuals emerge in various societies at different times of tension and conflict. Possibly the most familiar such historical episode is that of the Russian *narodniki*. These young students of the late nineteenth century came from a privileged stratum of their society and were overwhelmed by guilt over the hapless Russian peasants. As a result, the students embraced revolutionary aims and terroristic methods. They, like Owen, were reacting not against conditions which impinged directly upon them, but to societal inequities which made their own positions psychologically intolerable. A not dissimilar picture can be drawn of comfortable white college students in the American civil rights movement in the 1960's.

The motivational factor most commonly affecting the middle-class radical immigrants was alienation, a condition which enveloped the majority. While the extent of the alienation was directly related to the background and experience of each individual radical, nonetheless they shared analogous symptoms.

The alienation that marked these immigrants was characterized by opposition to governmental policies, disillusionment with traditional politics, and impatience with the slow rate of social progress. These alienated intellectuals came to repudiate the existing system, rejecting conventional values and beliefs, and condemning as irrational the course of material growth. Their pessimism over the prospects of meaningful change was especially pervasive among those from Central or Eastern Europe. They were hostile to existing institutions and yet did not see that political action or other strategies might make a difference. Even to try to promote change appeared hopeless. No effective channels for political and social improvements existed, and therefore impatience and frustration bred a sense of irresponsibility to the existing order.[2]

These alienated individuals believed that their choice lay between emigration and revolution. They could move to more fertile soil or they could remain and seek to undermine and destroy the system. The perspective they developed was a combination of their reaction to societal phenomena, including technical change, and their own individual psyches. Clearly, not all critics became alienated. Therefore, "... alienation was a product of the inner world and the outer world as they continually interacted in the developing individual's experience."[3]

The activist immigrants from the British Isles in the antebellum period were not wholly alienated from their society. In general, they accepted the freedoms of the English and American political institutions, favoring expansion of voting and civil rights. Their disillusionment stemmed from their economic and social perspectives. A number of them sought to construct their own just societies apart from the rest of the world.

The Forty-eighters originally lacked the political freedoms which the English immigrants took for granted. Therefore, when they settled in the United States, they brought with them political as well as economic and social discontent. The anger of these displaced Germans over their inability to build a constitutional and equitable nation in the Old World was dissipated in the exhilaration of the exercise of freedoms of the press, speech, and assembly and universal manhood suffrage which they found in the United States. Their initial alienation, much more potent than that of the English radicals, was tempered by American institutions. And while some of them never ceased to yearn for the radicalization of the United States, none attempted to undermine forcefully the existing structure. A Hassaurek and a Schurz entered politics. Those of a more revolutionary persuasion, the radical republican Heinzen and the Marxist Weydemeyer, utilized the American forum for propaganda purposes. They were no longer caught between the extremes of abandoning their hopes or smashing dominant institutions. The new environment modified their sense of alienation.

The labor militants and scientific revolutionaries who came to the United States late in the nineteenth century were, for the most part, products of rigid, inflexible societies. The depth of their pessimism and frustration induced a pervasive contempt for the political and economic institutions which they found here. They were bent on worldwide revolution, the need for which they took for granted, and their fixed views made it difficult for them to transcend superficial judgments. So colored was their vision by the alienation which had enveloped them, that they could not perceive subtle differences. While they were capable of insightful critiques, they often misconstrued the nature of the American system. All liberal states based on the private enterprise system seemed to them unjust and repressive. Escape from alienation was almost impossible for an Alexander Berkman and a Johann Most.

The beliefs of the radical immigrants cut across the leftist spectrum and reflect the period in which the individuals lived. The mid-century proved to be the watershed for the radicals' evaluation of the promise of America. Prior to that time, radical immigrants viewed the United States in decidedly positive terms. This country seemed to offer a hospitable climate for social experimentation and reform. Its unsettled physical environment and its flexible intellectual outlook were thought to provide the perfect framework for radical social programming. The attraction of America, when contrasted with the tired and corrupt Old World, was irresistible.

After the middle of the nineteenth century, the radicals' evaluation of the United States underwent a profound change. The developing and maturing nation no longer had available for social experimentation vast, isolated territories. Moreover, the American outlook was thought to be less open to the introduction of new ideas. But the settling of the country and its industrial development had brought new opportunities for the radical immigrants. The teeming cities, the social problems, and the incipient class conflict provided a new kind of challenge for radical immigrants. The tension and the conflict were seen by the latter-day revolutionaries as certain to result in a social explosion after which a new society of brotherhood and equality could be built.

The Marxists especially, through their theoretical framework, based on a belief in the dialectical process of history, saw great potential in the United States following the Haymarket Affair of 1886. This conflagration had convinced them that the capitalist development of America would soon result in violent social disruption. American prosperity clearly did not encompass the worker who was experiencing constant degradation. At the same time, American political freedom and democratic procedures failed to lead to an independent citizenry. The United States had proved "... the uselessness of democratic political institutions unless accompanied by social equality and social cooperation." The Marxist immigrants came to believe that the United States, through the increasing centralization of economic forces, was entering the advanced stage of capitalism which would result in its becoming the first socialist nation.[4]

In the course of the century of immigration discussed within these pages, various radicals shared some basic assumptions. Despite differences in ideology and period, a number of common threads mark their social vision. First, as children of the Enlightenment they believed that environment shaped the individual, and that neither government nor religion should limit human potential. Men and women must enjoy freedom in the widest sense. They must be fully emancipated so that they can determine their own destinies. Thus, most of the radicals preferred representative government based on popular sovereignty and universal suffrage. Secondly, the radicals, both in the Old World and the New, expanded. the fundamental definition of popular sovereignty beyond its eighteenth-century meaning to include citizen control of the economy. Without that significant variable, sovereignty was a delusion.[5]

Building within such a framework, the radical immigrants

further agreed on a number of specific criticisms. They believed that the policies and procedures of the American government tended to subvert the interests of the populace. Further, they agreed that the system of exchange was inequitable. Western liberalism was held to be inadequate if not wrong-headed. New political, economic, and social institutions were required, involving for most of the radicals the abandonment of some types of private property and the substitution of forms of collectivism.

Some extended their commitment to ideals of democracy and equality even to women. But in one area almost all the radicals failed in their demand for equality. Radical immigrants provided implicit support for American racism in their aloofness from the injustice of black oppression. This one social problem consistently escaped their attention as a result of their own racism or, for some, of their Marxist perspective. At the mid-century, Heinzen was the only radical to demand full equality for blacks. Of the later revolutionaries, the Marxists failed to recognize the special dilemma of black citizens, whom they saw as primarily workers. Only Emma Goldman focused upon the plight of black men and women in the United States.

The general commitment to democracy was violated again and again by the elitism to which the radicals were prone. This inegalitarian streak appeared consistently and was not limited to Marxists who specifically endorsed the concepts of a vanguard of the revolution or a dictatorship of the proletariat. Elitism was demonstrated in the paternalism of the communitarians, in the leadership of would-be labor spokesmen such as Thomas Brothers and Johann Most, and in the authoritarianism of Daniel DeLeon. Often basic behavioral patterns belied the theoretical belief in democracy.

Radicals of all stripes endorsed industrialization. Even those who embraced agrarianism at some point in their careers, viewed industrialization as symbolic of the progress of civilization. None supported a reversion to an unhurried, less cluttered preindustrial era. In their acceptance of industrialization, however, they all demanded that the fruits of industry be used to benefit the lives of the masses.

Finally, most of the radical immigrants were avowed internationalists, eschewing nationalism as a dangerous doctrine that arbitrarily divided humanity. There were some exceptions, such as a number of the Forty-eighters. But for the most part, the radical immigrants spoke in the interest of mankind as they saw it and consequently condemned nationalism and supported international solidarity and peace.

These radicals were products of their own times, despite alienation from their societies. Thus, in their beliefs they demonstrated blind spots symptomatic of their era. They were driven to radicalism most fundamentally as a reaction against the impact of mechanization and the resulting social upheaval which they observed. But, living in a period of increasing state power, these dissidents tended to find salvation through turning more power over to government. While the governments which they attacked had failed to alleviate poverty, suffering, and injustice, nevertheless the radicals, as a reflection of existing values, thought in terms of withholding power from selfish private interests and strengthening centralized authority. Only the anarchists were conspicuous exceptions to this approach. All the rest fell before the altar of a powerful central government.

Contributions made by the radical immigrants to the United States were varied. Sometimes they reinforced existing reform or radical movements and, at other times, they introduced fresh issues. As a whole, through their diffuse and at times distorted perspectives, they added new dimensions to the American struggle for social change and to American history.

In the early national period, foreign-born reformers transformed the religious communitarian movement into a secular struggle to create a just and egalitarian society. Other immigrants addressed themselves to the problems of the workers and began to teach Americans class awareness. These immigrant radicals were convinced of the callousness of the laissez-faire attitude of the American government toward the public, and they succeeded in leading workers to demand socially responsible policies. Workers supported various reforms, including agrarianism, a free public school system, and an amorphous type of collectivism, and they played a significant role in winning acceptance of an extension of the idea of the general welfare.

In the middle of the nineteenth century, during the height of the slavery controversy, defeated European revolutionaries brought to the United States additional support for abolitionism. The immigrant radicals perceived more clearly than native Americans the folly of compromise and the extent to which the controversy was disrupting the country. These radicals, opposing slavery even from within the South, sought to create new abolitionist alliances and strategems and demanded emancipation in concert with wide political and economic reforms. So determined were they to eradicate the "peculiar institution" that they were among the earliest supporters of the Free-Soil and the Republican parties and were among those who deserted Lincoln during the Civil War. These immigrant abolitionists sought to convince Americans that the moral issue was more significant than the survival of the Republic.

After the Civil War newcomers were quick to recognize deep polarization in society and the discrepancies between the unlimited American dreams of the past and the dark reality of the industrial era. Free from indigenous beliefs and traditions, the radical immigrants of these decades demanded political, economic, and social reforms in new directions. In the footsteps of a few antebellum and Forty-eighter radicals, they argued that working conditions demanded class consciousness and collective action.

The immigrants emphasized that only unity could insure workers' rights in the face of the increasing strength of capital. Divisions based on skill, nationality, or color must be abandoned. The tight social structure of some of the immigrants from Eastern Europe and the educated leadership and community traditions of the Jewish immigrant workers helped cement collective action and served as an example to the rank-and-file native workers. Immigrant radicals proposed militant weapons, such as industrial unionism, the general strike, and political parties to represent the workers. Marxist and anarchist revolutionaries exhorted the masses to prepare to assume their rightful control of the political and economic system of the country. The liberal American system, they maintained, had failed to serve their interests. Revolution, not reform, was their solution to the social question.

In the century of argument and propaganda by radical immigrants Americans did not always prove to be a receptive audience. Indeed, often the radicals found ·listeners only in their own circles. At other times, however, especially during great upheavals, as in the 1850's and 1880's, the radicals did succeed in impressing some of their ideas on the public mind. Ideas of foreign origin did penetrate the American mainstream.

The legacy of these immigrant radicals is twofold. First, they brought enormous vigor to the various social struggles of American life, expanding the vistas of every battle which they joined. Secondly, their presence served constantly to challenge the American constitutional commitment to freedom of speech. In each era, these radicals faced persecution and prosecution for unconventional and unpopular views, from locked lecture halls to federal indictments. Their undaunted perseverance almost always brought them eventual vindication by the court system, except in the darkest days of the Red Scare deportations.

The saga of the radical immigrant, with his pronounced beliefs, strong motivation, and distinctive contributions, ended a half century ago. Yet until now his history had not been written; he has not been seen in his own light. Oscar Handlin has stated that American history cannot be accurately evaluated with the immigrant segregated from it. The immigrants form the history of the United States. And the radicals among them played a special role, adding an extra dimension to American history.

Notes and References

CHAPTER I

1. Frank Thistlethwaite, "Migration from Europe Overseas in the Nineteenth and Twentieth Centuries," in *New Perspectives on the American Past*, II, eds. Stanley N. Katz and Stanley I. Kutler (Boston, 1969), 57-65.

2. See E. P. Thompson, *The Making of the English Working Class* (London, 1963).

3. Economic rather than political factors stimulated emigration. In 1846 and 1847, 100,000 people left the German states each year for overseas destinations. In that decade, one-half million emigrated. Theodore S. Hamerow, *Restoration, Revolution, Reaction: Economics and Politics in Germany, 1815-1871* (Princeton, 1967), pp. 82-83, 208-9; Marcus L. Hansen, "The Revolutions of 1848 and German Emigration," *Journal of Economic and Business History*, II (1930), 653-56.

4. Maldwyn A. Jones, *American Immigration* (Chicago, 1960), p. 198.

5. Carl Wittke, *We Who Built America* (rev. ed.; Cleveland, 1967), pp. 409-10; Moses Rischin, *The Promised City: New York's Jews, 1870-1914* (New York, 1970), pp. 19, 24, 45-46; Samuel Joseph, *Jewish Immigration to the United States* (New York, 1914), pp. 53-55, 121-23.

6. United States Immigration Commission, *Report of the Immigration Commission: 1907-1910*, I, 63.

7. Thistlethwaite, p. 69; Rowland Tappan Berthoff, *British Immigrants in Industrial America, 1790-1950* (Cambridge, Mass., 1953), pp. 28-29.

8. See Jones, chapter 9.

9. See John Higham, *Strangers in the Land: Patterns of American Nativism, 1860-1925* (New York, 1925) for the most comprehensive consideration of nativism.

10. Edward N. Saveth, *American Historians and European Immigrants, 1875-1925* (New York, 1965), pp. 200-203.

11. O. Fritiof Ander, "Four Historians of Immigration," in O. Fritiof Ander, *In the Trek of the Immigrants: Essays Presented To Carl Wittke* (Rock Island, Illinois, 1964), pp. 20-24.

12. Oscar Handlin, *The Uprooted: The Epic Story of the Great Migrations that Made the American People* (New York, 1951), pp. 108-10.

13. For examples of such revisionist scholarship, see Rudolph J. Vecoli, "Contadini in Chicago: A Critique of *The Uprooted*," *Journal of American History*, LIV (1964), 404-17; Victor R. Greene, *The Slavic Community on Strike: Immigrant Labor in Anthracite* (Notre Dame, 1968).

CHAPTER II

1. On social change and the working class, see especially E. P. Thompson, *The Making of the English Working Class* (London, 1963), p. 198, and Eric Hobsbawm, *Primitive Rebels* (New York, 1965), p. 3.

2. Robert Dale Owen, *Threading My Way* (New York, 1874), pp. 240-41.

3. John R. Commons, *History of Labour in the United States* (New York, 1918), I, 153-56; Norman Ware, *The Industrial Worker, 1840-1860* (Chicago, 1964), p. 36.

4. *New Harmony Gazette*, November 8, 1826, p. 46.

5. Arthur Bestor, *Backwoods Utopias: the Sectarian and Owenite Phases of Communitarian Socialism in America, 1663-1829* (Philadelphia, 1950), p. 60; Richard W. Leopold, *Robert Dale Owen: a Biography* (Cambridge, Massachusetts, 1940), pp. 26-27. These two historians offer contrasting emphases on the value of the insights of foreign-born reformers in the 1820's.

6. Owen, pp. 264-65; Robert Dale Owen, *To Holland and to New Harmony: Robert Dale Owen's Travel Diary, 1825-1826*, ed. Josephine M. Elliott, Indiana Historical Society Publications, XXIII (Indianapolis, 1969), 231-32.

7. Owen, *To Holland and to New Harmony*, pp. 240-51. The passenger list on the keelboat, named the *Philanthropist* and nicknamed the "boatload of knowledge," included William Maclure, educator, zoologist, and Robert Owen's financial partner in New Harmony; C. A. Lesueur, artist and naturalist, and Thomas Say, entomologist, both of the Academy of Natural Sciences; Marie Duclos Fretageot and William Phiquepal d'Arusmont, Pestalozzian-trained teachers; M. Chase, chemist; Gerald Troost, chemist and zoologist; and Cornelius Tiebout, artist and engraver. (Extant passenger lists conflict but these names appear on most lists.) Arthur Bestor, in describing this transfer of some of Philadelphia's cultural leadership to New Harmony, calls it one of the significant intellectual migrations in history. Bestor, pp. 133-34.

8. Robert Dale Owen to his mother, August 12, 1830, New York, Robert Owen Papers, Library Co-operative Union Ltd., Manchester, England; Frances Wright to Mrs. Robert Owen, February 9, 1828, Memphis, *ibid.* In this letter Frances Wright assured Robert Dale's mother that he would thrive in an uncompetitive microcosm of the larger society, no matter how rough-hewn the conditions might be.

9. Leopold, p. 7; Owen, *Threading My Way*, pp. 126-27, 270.

10. Owen, *Threading My Way*, pp. 147-69.

11. Owen, *To Holland and to New Harmony*, p. 248; Nicholas V. Riasanovsky, *The Teaching of Charles Fourier* (Berkeley, 1969), pp. 70-81. Riasanovsky, unlike so many others, treats Fourier in terms of his own system of thought rather than in its relationship to those of others.

12. Owen, *Threading My Way*, p. 201; Bestor, p. 143.

13. Leopold, p. 5; Frank Podmore, *Robert Owen, a Biography* (New York, 1924), II, 644; *New Harmony Gazette*, November 12, 1825, p. 51. Robert Dale Owen's "Outline of the System of Education at New-Lanark" was serialized in the first issues of the *Gazette*.

14. Robert Owen to Reverend Mr. George Rapp, August 4, 1820, New Lanark, Eben Lane Papers, Chicago Historical Society. John F. C. Harrison in *Quest for the New Moral World: Robert Owen and the Owenites in Britain and America* (New York, 1969), p. 54, offers 1815 as a date by which Owen was clearly familiar with religious sectarianism in the United States.

15. Owen, *Threading My Way*, pp. 240-41; Robert Owen to William Allen, April 21, 1825, New Harmony, Robert Owen Papers, Library Co-operative Union Ltd., Manchester, England.

16. Bestor, pp. 4, 38, 57. To avoid ambiguity, Arthur Bestor has argued for utilization of the term "communitarianism" to designate such small, reformist colonies, as distinct from the term "communism" which implies more than the collective holding of property. See p. viii. Also, see John Humphrey Noyes, *American Socialisms* (Philadelphia, 1870), p. 30.

17. *New Harmony Gazette*, October 1, 1825, p. 1, May 10, 1826, p. 262, June 7, 1826, p. 294. These issues printed the addresses of Robert Owen to the community on April 27, 1825, May 9, 1826, and May 28, 1826, respectively. William Owen begged his father to discourage potential immigrants to New Harmony, but Robert Owen publicized the overcrowded community wherever he went, William Owen to Robert Owen, December 16, 1825, New Harmony, Robert Owen Papers, Library Co-operative Union Ltd., Manchester, England.

18. Owen, *Threading My Way*, pp. 276-84; "Miner K. Kellogg:

Recollections of New Harmony," ed. Lorna Lutes Sylvester, *Indiana Magazine of History*, LXIV (March, 1968), 50-52.

19. *New Harmony Gazette*, October 1, 1825, p. 1.

20. *Ibid.*, April 2, 1828, pp. 180-81, as an example of pedagogical interests.

21. Albert Post, *Popular Free Thought in America, 1825-50* (New York, 1943), pp. 34-38.

22. *New Harmony Gazette*, November 8, pp. 46-47, November 15, p. 54, November 22, p. 62, November 29, p. 70, December 6, p. 79, December 13, 1826, pp. 86-87.

23. Owen, *Threading My Way*, p. 285.

24. See *New Harmony Gazette*, February 15, 1826, pp. 161-62 for the constitution. Owen, *Threading My Way*, p. 287; Bestor, pp. 172-73.

25. Bestor, pp. 116-18, 179; Podmore, I, 291; William E. Wilson, *The Angel and the Serpent* (Bloomington, 1964), pp. 101-2; Noyes, p. 56; Owen, *Threading My Way*, p. 259. Owen's residences at New Harmony were from December 16, 1824 to January 3, 1825, April 13, 1825, to June 5, 1825, and January 12, 1826, to June 1, 1827. The fleetingness of Owen's American residence precluded consideration of Owen as an immigrant although his biographer indicates that in May, 1825, he announced his intention of becoming an American citizen. Podmore, I, 327. See Bestor (pp. 260-64) for his questioning the appropriateness of the frontier for communitarian experiments geared to the problems of industrial society.

26. *New Harmony Gazette*, December 16, 1828, p. 78, March 28, 1827, p. 206, March 26, 1828, p. 174; Owen, *Threading My Way*, p. 289. At the demise of the parent colony, two satellite colonies remained autonomous.

27. Owen, *Threading My Way*, p. 360.

28. Frances Wright, *Biography and Notes of Frances Wright* (New York, 1844), p. 11; Frances Wright, *Views of Society and Manners in America*, ed. Paul R. Baker (Cambridge, Massachusetts, 1963), p. 211; William Randall Waterman, *Frances Wright*, Columbia University Studies in History, Economics, and Public Law, CXV (1924), 41; Amos Gilbert, *Memoir of Frances Wright: the Pioneer Woman in the Cause of Human Rights* (Cincinnati, 1855), p. 23; Frances Wright to Matthew Carey, February 1, 1820, New York, August 10, 1820, Cumberland, England, Edward Carey Gardiner Collection, Historical Society of Pennsylvania. After her first visit she wanted the American people to know ". . . that they have had at least one traveller among them who could see, acknowledge and rejoice in the choice blessings that Heaven has conferred on them. . . ."

29. Frances Wright to Albert Gallatin, Paris, October 21, 1821, Box 24, Letter 84, Albert Gallatin Collection, New-York Historical Society; Wright, *Biography*, p. 15.

30. *New Harmony Gazette*, October 1, 1828, p. 389; *Free Enquirer*, March 4, 1829, pp. 145-47; Frances Wright, *Course of Popular Lectures* (6th ed.; New York, 1836), Lecture 1, pp. 6-10, Lecture 5, pp. 108-10.

31. Wright, *Biography*, pp. 29-30.

32. Gilbert, p. 33; *New Harmony Gazette*, February 6, 1828, p. 133.

33. *New Harmony Gazette*, February 6, 1828, p. 132, January 30, 1828, p. 125; Wright, *Biography*, pp. 24-28. Robert Dale Owen's diary indicates that that combination was suggested to Robert Owen prior to his organizing New Harmony in early 1826.

34. Frances Wright visited "Harmonie" under the German Rappites and also visited their second community, Economy, Pennsylvania, each of which prospered but seemed intellectually stultifying to her. She had the same reaction to the Shakers' community. Nonreligious settlements she visited included those under abolitionist George Flower and Morris Birkbeck in southern Illinois. The latter were not organized cooperatively but showed that homogeneity and goodwill could effectively turn wilderness into civilization. See Jane Rodman, "The English Settlement in Southern Illinois, 1815-1825," *Indiana Magazine of History*, XLIII (1947), 329-61.

35. Wright, *Biography*, pp. 22-24; O. B. Emerson, "Frances Wright and Her Nashoba Experiment," *Tennessee Historical Quarterly*, VI (1947), 292-94.

36. *New Harmony Gazette*, February 6, 1828, pp. 132-33.

37. *New Harmony Gazette*, October 1, 1825, pp. 4-5, February 21, 1827, p. 164. The ten members of the board of trustees included Robert Dale Owen, William Maclure, and Robert Jennings of New Harmony, and George Flower of Illinois.

38. *New Harmony Gazette*, March 26, 1828, p. 172. The first phrase is from a letter of Frances Wright to Mrs. Robert Owen, February 9, 1828, Nashoba, Robert Owen Papers, Library Cooperative Union Ltd., Manchester, England, and the second phrase is Robert Dale Owen's in *Threading My Way*, p. 299. Noyes likens the symbiotic relationship of the races at Nashoba to ancient Greece. Noyes, p. 68.

39. Owen, *Threading My Way*, pp. 301-3.

40. William Owen to Robert Dale Owen, New Harmony, August 22, 1827, Robert Dale Owen Collection, Indiana State Library; Frances Wright to Robert Dale Owen, London, October 2, 1827, Ferdinand J. Dreer Collection, Pennsylvania Historical Society.

41. Wright, *Biography,* pp. 31-33; Waterman, p. 120.

42. Albert Shaw, *Icaria: A Chapter in the History of Communism* (New York, 1884), pp. 19-20; G. D. H. Cole, *The Forerunners,* Vol. I of *A History of Socialist Thought* (New York, 1965), 76-77.

43. See Etienne Cabet, "The History of the Colony or Republic of Icaria in the United States of America," in *Socialism in America: From the Shakers to the Third International, A Documentary History,* ed. Albert Fried (New York, 1970), p. 173; Shaw, pp. 12-15. Shaw, among other writers, considers Cabet a disciple of Owen's. After the two met in 1847, at which time Owen probably suggested Texas as a likely area of colonization based on his own visit there, Cabet decided to found a colony in the United States. See Shaw, pp. 22-23.

44. Cabet in Fried, pp. 170-72; Shaw, pp. 47-52.

45. Shaw, pp. 53-60; Nordhoff, p. 335; Mark Holloway, *Heavens on Earth: Utopian Communities in America, 1680-1880* (New York, 1966), pp. 204-8.

46. Arthur E. Bestor, "Albert Brisbane—Propagandist for Socialism in the 1840's," *New York History,* XXVIII (April, 1947), 134-38.

47. *Ibid.,* 140, 145.

48. Ware, pp. 164-65.

49. Bestor, *Backwoods Utopias,* p. 227. Also see Bestor's "Supplementary Essay, II," pp. 253-71 in the second edition.

50. Rowland Tappan Berthoff, *British Immigrants in Industrial America, 1790-1950* (Cambridge, Massachusetts, 1953), pp. 21-29, 127. Up to 1870, two-thirds of the immigrants to the United States were British, although in some decades they were mainly Irish.

51. Commons, I, 175.

52. Berthoff, pp. 88-90; Walter Hugins, *Jacksonian Democracy and the Working Class: A Study of the New York Workingmen's Movement, 1829-1837* (Stanford, 1960), p. 109; Clifton K. Yearley, Jr., *Britons in American Labor: A History of the Influence of the United Kingdom Immigrants in American Labor, 1820-1914* (Baltimore, 1957), p. 45. Berthoff notes inherent difficulties in tracing English participation and contributions to American life since such immigrants blended in easier than others, but Hugins's utilization of quantitative methodology allows him to identify activists with greater precision than could earlier students. Hugins finds that one-third of the leaders in New York were from the British Isles.

53. Louis H. Arky, "The Mechanics' Union of Trade Associations and the Formation of the Philadelphia Workingmen's Movement," *Pennsylvania Magazine of History and Biography,* LXXI (April, 1952), 144.

54. *Ibid.,* 148-53, 171-73. See the *Workingmen's Advocate* of

November 28, 1829, February 13, 1830, and March 6, 1830, for excerpts from the *Mechanics' Free Press* endorsing elementary education as an avenue to the collective advancement of the working class.

55. *Radical Reformer and Working Man's Advocate,* June 27, 1835, p. 33; Thomas Brothers to the Chartists, August 9, 1839, p. 222, Brothers to Thomas C. Cope, June 1, 1839, in Thomas Brothers, *The United States of North America as They Are, Not As They Are Generally Described,* p. 81; Cole, I, 113.

56. Edward Pessen, *Most Uncommon Jacksonians: The Radical Leaders of the Early Labor Movement* (Albany, 1967), p. 81.

57. *Radical Reformer and Working Man's Advocate,* August 22, 1835, p. 162, July 4, 1835, p. 49.

58. Thomas Brothers to his sons, May 25, 1838, Brothers to the Rt. Honourable Earl Stanhope, July 30, 1839, Brothers to Thomas Attwood, July 15, 1839, Brothers to the Chartists, August 9, 1839, in Brothers, pp. 121, 149, 58, 260.

59. *Ibid.* October 31, 1829.

60. Lewis Masquerier, *Sociology: or the Reconstruction of Society, Government, and Property* (New York, 1877), p. 99; "George Henry Evans," *Dictionary of American Biography,* VI, 201-2; Yearley, p. 37; F. Byrdsall, *The History of the Loco-Foco or Equal Rights Party: Its Movements, Conventions and Proceedings With Short Characteristic Sketches of its Prominent Men* (New York, 1867), p. 15.

61. Ware, p. 181; Cole, I, 24. Thomas Skidmore (see below) also was familiar with the writings of Thomas Spence. See Pessen, pp. 148-49.

62. Frederick William Evans, *Autobiography of a Shaker* (New York, 1869), pp. 10-30; Post, pp. 69-70; Masquerier, p. 96. In the *Working Man's Advocate* of December 12, 1829, Evans felt it necessary to deny any interest in the overthrow of "social, moral, and religious institutions of the United States."

63. Helen S. Zahler, *Eastern Workingmen and National Land Policy, 1829-1862* (New York, 1941), p. 22.

64. *Working Man's Advocate,* October 31, November 14, 1829; *Man,* May 12, February 22, March 25, March 22, and March 31, 1834.

65. *Man,* May 12, May 3, February 18, 1834.

66. *Working Man's Advocate,* October 31, 1829; November 7, 1829; Commons, I, 235; George Henry Evans, "Of the Origin and Progress of the Working Men's Party in New York," *Radical in Continuation of the Working Man's Advocate,* January, 1842, pp. 2-4, 8-9.

67. The agrarianism of the New York workingmen's movement may be directly related to the Connecticut-born Thomas Skidmore

(1800-1832), who dominated party policy in its first six months. While historians debate whether or not the rank and file of the movement understood the implications of agrarianism's attack on private property, nevertheless the subject of land redistribution was prominent in the early meetings. Commons, I, 245; Pessen, pp. 62-65, 150-52; *Working Man's Advocate,* October 31, 1829.

68. Robert Dale Owen played an influential role behind the scenes. At this time he edited anonymously the *Daily Sentinel,* and his writings injected the issue of education into the labor movement. He was more convinced than ever that education was the key to erasing political and socioeconomic inequities. He sponsored the so-called National System of Education where children would be educated and housed at government expense. "Robert Dale Owen," *Dictionary of American Biography,* XIV, 118-20, traces his later, more conventional, political career. As a state legislator in Indiana and as a Congressman, he strengthened the legal position of women, helped settle the Oregon boundary dispute, and introduced a bill to organize the Smithsonian Institute. He ended his career as a diplomat and spiritualist.

69. *Free Enquirer,* October 31, 1829, p. 7; *Working Man's Advocate,* October 31, 1829, January 16, 1830.

70. *Ibid.,* November 14, 1829; Pessen, 74; *Daily Sentinel,* May 3, April 10, 1830.

71. *Working Man's Advocate,* May 18, December 21, July 24, 1844.

72. Masquerier, p. 101.

73. Zahler, p. 177.

74. *Working Man's Advocate,* November 6, 1830; Commons, I, 177.

75. Hugins, p. 110.

76. Pessen, p. 63; Commons, I, 245.

77. Yearley, pp. 314-17.

78. See, for example, Aileen S. Kraditor, ed. *Up From the Pedestal: Selected Writings in the History of American Feminism* (Chicago, 1968), p. 8.

79. *Free Enquirer,* September 23, 1829, p. 382; October 31, 1829, p. 1; Wright, *Biography,* p. 40; Waterman, p. 134.

80. Frances Trollope, *Domestic Manners of the Americans,* ed. Donald Smalley (New York, 1949), p. 71.

81. *Diary of Philip Hone,* ed. Allan Nevins (New York, 1927), I, 9-10; Frances Wright to Dr. Ducatel, March 2, 1829, New York, Ferdinand J. Dreer Collection, Historical Society of Pennsylvania.

82. Sara A. Underwood, *Heroines of Free Thought* (New York, 1876), p. 220; Margaret Lane, *Frances Wright and the "Great Experiment"* (Manchester, 1972), pp. 30-32.

83. Frances Wright as quoted in Gilbert, p. 73.

84. *Free Enquirer,* April 1, 1829, p. 177.

85. *Ibid.,* March 4, 1829, p. 151, April 29, 1829, p. 213. Married women were never as helpless within the American legal system as were English wives in theirs. Wealthy Americans invariably protected their daughters' inheritances by trusts or other measures. See Andrew Sinclair, *The Better Half: The Emancipation of the American Woman* (New York, 1965), pp. 83-87.

86. *New Harmony Gazette,* September 10, 1828, p. 366; *Free Enquirer,* December 3, 1828, p. 40.

87. *New Harmony Gazette,* July 2, 1828, p. 286; *Free Enquirer,* May 13, 1829, p. 225.

88. "Ernestine Rose," *Dictionary of American Biography,* XVI, 158-59; Yuri Suhl, *Ernestine Rose and the Battle for Human Rights* (New York, 1959), pp. 10-16.

89. Underwood, pp. 266-68; *Dictionary of American Biography,* XVI, 158-59.

90. *Dictionary of American Biography,* XVI, 158-59; Suhl, pp. 90, 170.

91. The extant fragments of her correspondence suggest both her frantic pace and her concern for the ideas for which she stood. For a glimpse of her split-second travel schedule, see her letters of December 23, 1854, December 26, 1854, January 2, 1855, January 12, 1855, and January 29, 1855, to Charles H. Plummer in the Vassar College Manuscript Collections. For her reformist commitment, see Ernestine Rose to Robert Dale Owen, December, 1844, Robert Owen Papers, Library Co-operative Union Ltd., Manchester, England.

92. Underwood, p. 256; *History of Women Suffrage,* I, 237-41.

93. Mathilde Anneke to Alexander Jonas, no date, "Biographical Notes in Commemoration of Fritz Anneke and Mathilde Franziska Giesler-Anneke," ed. Hertha Anneke Sanne and Henriette M. Heinzen, p. 35, Fritz Anneke and Mathilde Franziska Giesler-Anneke Papers, State Historical Society of Wisconsin.

94. Dora Edinger, "A Feminist Forty-eighter," *The American-German Review,* XXXVIII (June, 1942), 18-19; A. B. Faust, "Mathilde Franzeska Giesler-Anneke: 'Memorien einer frau aus dem badish-pfalzischer feldzug,' and a sketch of her career," *German-American Annals,* XVI, N.S. (May-August, 1918), 78-79. Among their friends were Marx, Engels, Freiligrath, Beust, and Kinkel.

95. Carl Wittke, *The German Language Press in America* (Lexington, 1957), pp. 162, 102; Mathilde Anneke to Alexander Jonas, no date, "Biographical Notes . . . ," p. 36, also p. 29, Fritz Anneke and Mathilde Franziska Giesler-Anneke Papers, Wisconsin State Historical Society.

96. Fritz Anneke to Mathilde Anneke, February 16, 1868; Mathilde Anneke to Fritz Anneke, February or March, 1868; Fritz Anneke to Mathilde Anneke, November 14, 1867, pp. 190-91, 199, Fritz Anneke and Mathilde Franziska Giesler-Anneke Papers, State Historical Society of Wisconsin.

97. Mathilde to Fritz Anneke, May 4, 1869, p. 206; Mathilde Anneke to ?, June 8, 1869, pp. 209-10, *ibid.*

98. "Biographical Notes . . . ," p. 185, *ibid.*

99. For a comparative analysis of native feminists, see Robert E. Riegel, *American Feminists* (Lawrence, Kansas, 1963), chapter 10.

CHAPTER III

1. It has been estimated that political emigrants numbered a few thousand among the one million Germans who emigrated in the decade following the Revolutions of 1848-49.

2. Emigration statistics demonstrate that adverse economic conditions were a greater causative factor than was the political question. See discussions in Theodore S. Hamerow, *Restoration, Revolution, Reaction: Economics and Politics in Germany, 1815-1871* (Princeton, 1967), pp. 82-83, 208-9, and in Marcus L. Hansen, "The Revolutions of 1848 and German Emigration," *Journal of Economic and Business History,* II (1930), 653-56.

3. Albert Bernhardt Faust, *The German Element in the United States with Special Reference to its Political, Moral, Social and Educational Influence* (Boston, 1909), I, 581; John Hawgood, *The Tragedy of German-America: the Germans in the United States of America During the Nineteenth Century—and After* (New York, 1940), pp. 44-50.

4. Hawgood, pp. 98-103.

5. Carl Wittke, *Refugees of Revolution: The German Forty-Eighters in America* (Philadelphia, 1952), pp. 9-14.

6. Hildegard Binder Johnson, "Adjustment to the United States," in *The Forty-Eighters: Political Refugees of the German Revolution of 1848,* ed. Adolf E. Zucker (New York, 1950), pp. 43-50; Ernest Bruncken, *German Political Refugees in the United States During the Period From 1815-1860* (1904), pp. 28-32. See "Biographical Dictionary of the Forty-Eighters" in Zucker, pp. 269-357. Zucker generalized that the typical political refugee was a young professional man from southwestern Germany.

7. Carl Wittke, *Against the Current: the Life of Karl Heinzen* (Chicago, 1945), p. v.

8. Carl Wittke, *The German-Language Press in America* (Lexington, 1957), pp. 113, 121; Wittke, *Against the Current,* pp. 92-93.

9. Wittke, *Against the Current*, pp. 1-7, 21-31.

10. *Ibid.*, pp. 33-35, 54-55; Zucker, *The Forty-Eighters*, pp. 302-3.

11. Karl Heinzen, *Teutscher Radikalismus in Amerika* (Boston, 1867), III, 47.

12. Karl Heinzen, *Erlebtes Zweiter Theil: Nach Meiner Exilirung* (Boston, 1874), II, 166; Karl Heinzen, *What Is Humanity?* (Indianapolis, 1877), pp. 4, 13-21.

13. Wittke, *Against the Current*, p. 199; Heinzen, *Teutscher Radikalismus in Amerika*, II, 216, III, 373-75; Heinzen, *What Is Real Democracy?* (Indianapolis, 1871), pp. 10-14, 19, 28, 39.

14. Karl Heinzen, *Murder and Liberty* (Indianapolis, 1881), p. 24. This pamphlet was reprinted at the turn of the century by anarchist Johann Most and resulted in his arrest following the assassination of President William McKinley (see below).

15. Heinzen, *Teutscher Radikalismus in Amerika*, III, 5-6; Wittke, *Against the Current*, pp. 164-66; Heinzen, *What Is Humanity?* p. 22; Hawgood, p. 231; L. Stierlin, *Der Staat Kentucky und die Stadt Louisville mit besonderer Berücksichtigung des Deutschen Elements* (Louisville, 1873), p. 64. A complete discussion of the Louisville Platform is found in Wittke.

16. Wittke, *Against the Current*, pp. 171-77.

17. Karl Heinzen, *The Rights of Women and the Sexual Relations* (Chicago, 1891), pp. 2-5, 36-38, 131; Heinzen, *Teutscher Radikalismus in Amerika*, III, 243; Wittke, *Against the Current*, pp. 132-34, 219-20.

18. Karl Heinzen, *Teutscher Radikalismus in Amerika*, I, 186.

19. *Ibid.*, I, 191; Wittke, *Against the Current*, 230, 236-42.

20. Wittke, *Against the Current*, p. 228.

21. Morris Hillquit, *History of Socialism in the United States* (New York, 1910), pp. 144-46; Carl Wittke, *The Utopian Communist: a Biography of Wilhelm Weitling* (Baton Rouge, 1950), pp. 16-23. The bulk of the published work on Weitling has dealt with his European career only. An early study of Weitling, upon which twentieth-century historians have built, must be judged carefully for errors abound: see Frederick C. Clark, "A Neglected Socialist," *Annals of the American Academy of Political and Social Science*, V (1895), 66-87.

22. Hillquit, pp. 145-47.

23. Herman Schlüter, *Die Anfänge der deutschen Arbeiterbewegung in Amerika* (Stuttgart, 1907), pp. 38-39, 120-21; *Die Republik der Arbeiter*, June 24, 1854, p. 1.; Wittke, *The Utopian Communist*, pp. 46-48.

24. *Die Republik der Arbeiter*, January, 1850, p. 11, p. 5; Schlüter, pp. 96, 100.

25. Robert Ernst, *Immigrant Life in New York City, 1825-1863* (New York, 1959), pp. 112-14; Wittke, *The Utopian Communist,* pp. 188-91.

26. *Die Republik der Arbeiter,* January, 1850, p. 6; Wittke, pp. 201-2; Schlüter, pp. 71-75.

27. Schlüter, pp. 87-88; Ernst, p. 117; Wittke, *The Utopian Communist,* p. 235.

28. Schlüter, p. 113.

29. *Die Republik der Arbeiter,* January, 1850, pp. 6-7; George Schulz-Behrend, "Communia, Iowa, a Nineteenth Century German-American Utopia," *Iowa Journal of History,* XLVIII (1950), 30, 34-36.

30. Schulz-Behrend, *Iowa Journal of History,* XLVIII, 41; Wilhelm Weitling to R. Kreter, July 20, 1852, Weitling to the Workingmen's League of St. Louis, July 21, 1852, Weitling to the Central Commission of the Workingmen's League of New York, July 14, 1853, Communia, in Wilhelm Weitling Collection, Folder 4, New York Public Library. See Folder 7 for a copy of the detailed but ambiguous constitution which Weitling persuaded Communia to adopt in 1853.

31. Karl Obermann, *Joseph Weydemeyer: Pioneer of American Socialism* (New York, 1947), pp. 11-13.

32. *Ibid.,* pp. 20-29; David Herreshoff, *American Disciples of Marx: From the Age of Jackson to the Progressive Era* (Detroit, 1967), pp. 54-56.

33. Friedrich A. Sorge, "Joseph Weydemeyer und sein Antheil an der deutschen Bewegung der vierziger Jahre und an der amerikanischen Bewegung der fünfziger Jahre," *Pionier* (1897), p. 54; Obermann, pp. 36, 49-51; Joseph Weydemeyer, "The Dictatorship of the Proletariat," *Turn-Zeitung,* January 1, 1852, p. 19.

34. Weydemeyer, *Turn-Zeitung,* January 1, 1852, p. 19; Hal Draper, "Joseph Weydemeyer's 'Dictatorship of the Proletariat,'" *Labor History,* III (1962), 208, 211-13.

35. Obermann, pp. 36, 63-64; Herreshoff, pp. 29-30, 62-64; John R. Commons, *History of Labour in the United States* (New York, 1918), I, 618-22.

36. Marx, Engels, and other German refugees abroad flooded Weydemeyer's various papers with articles and essays. One of Weydemeyer's sporadically appearing sheets was the original publisher of Marx's "18th Brumaire of Louis Bonaparte." Obermann, p. 39.

37. Friedrich Kapp to Joseph Weydemeyer, November 17, 1865, New York, Joseph Weydemeyer Collection, Library of Congress. Weydemeyer was elected county auditor in St. Louis and in that office sought stringent tax laws. Herreshoff, pp. 66-67.

38. Maldwyn A. Jones, *American Immigration* (Chicago, 1960), pp. 162-64; Hawgood, p. 50.

39. Bruncken, pp. 43-45.

40. Stierlin, *Der Staat Kentucky* ... , p. 187; Wittke, *Against the Current*, pp. 91-92.

41. A. E. Zucker, "Carl Heinrich Schnauffer," *Proceedings of the Annual Meeting of the Society for the History of Germans in Maryland* (1939), pp. 21-22; Dieter Cunz, *The Maryland Germans: A History* (Princeton, 1948), pp. 259-60. Schnauffer was not the only immigrant journalist whose abolitionist crusade threatened him with the destruction and death visited on Elijah Lovejoy in southern Illinois. Georg Schneider, editor of the most influential German daily, the *Illinois Staatszeitung*, was forced out of St. Louis when a mob destroyed his newspaper, the *Neue Zeit*, in 1850. Adolf Douai, in southwestern Texas, also lost his newspaper and was fortunate to avoid personal assault.

42. Schnauffer, like Tyrtaeus, the elegiac poet-soldier of ancient Greece, was the bard of his homeland at war. Zucker, *Proceedings*, 17-18; Dieter Cunz, "Carl Heinrich Schnauffers Literarische Versuche," *Publications of the Modern Language Association of America*, LIX (1944), 526; Dieter Cunz, "The Baltimore Germans and the Year 1848," *The American German Review*, X (1943), 33; Cunz, *The Maryland Germans*, pp. 276-81.

43. Hawgood, pp. 190-91; Rudolph Leopold Biesele, *The History of the German Settlements in Texas, 1831-1861* (Austin, 1930), pp. 133-35.

44. Biesele, pp. 195-204; Rudolph Leopold Biesele, "The Texas State Convention of Germans in 1854," *Southwestern Historical Quarterly*, XXXIII (1930), 248-51; Laura Wood Roper, "Frederick Law Olmsted and the Western Texas Free-Soil Movement," *American Historical Review*, LVI (1950), 58-59.

45. Biesele, *Southwestern Historical Quarterly*, XXXIII, 256-61; Roper, pp. 58-59.

46. Adolf Douai to F. L. Olmsted and J. H. Olmsted, February 9, 1855, San Antonio, Douai to J. H. Olmsted, September 4, 1854, San Antonio, Frederick Law Olmsted Collection, Library of Congress.

47. Adolf Douai to J. H. Olmsted, September 4, 1854, San Antonio, Frederick Law Olmsted Collection, Library of Congress; Adolf Douai, *Land und Leute in der Union* (Berlin, 1864), p. 282.

48. Frederick Law Olmsted, *Journey Through Texas: A Saddle-Trip on the Southwestern Frontier*, ed. James Howard (Austin, 1962), p. 104; Adolf Douai to Frederick Law Olmsted, December 7, 1854, San Antonio, Frederick Law Olmsted Collection, Library of Congress.

49. Adolf Douai to F. L. Olmsted, February 9 and August 4, 1855, San Antonio, Douai to F. L. Olmsted, October 28, 1854, San

Antonio, Frederick Law Olmsted Collection, Library of Congress; Roper, p. 61.

50. Douai, *Land und Leute in der Union,* pp. 125, 32-33; see Douai in Zucker, *The Forty-Eighters,* pp. 288-89.

51. F. I. Herriott, "The Conference in the Deutsches Haus, Chicago, May 14-15, 1860: A Study of Some of the Preliminaries of the National Republican Convention of 1860," *Transactions of the Illinois State Historical Society,* XXXV (1928), 107; Faust, II, 135.

52. Faust, II, 128-30; Bruncken, pp. 43-45.

53. Bruncken, p. 45; Hawgood, p. 246; Faust, II, 131.

54. Hawgood, pp. 249-50; Herriott, *Transactions . . . ,* XXXV, 109. James Bergquist argues that the Germans played a significant role in the avoidance of nativism by the national Republican party. See Bergquist, "People and Politics in Transition: the Illinois Germans, 1850-1860," in *Ethnic Voters and the Election of Lincoln,* ed. Frederick C. Luebke (Lincoln, Nebraska, 1971), p. 207. Bergquist also cautions against viewing the Germans in the United States as a homogeneous group at this time, pp. 198-201.

55. Herriott, *Transactions . . . ,* XXXV, 89.

56. *Ibid.,* 106; Lawrence S. Thompson and Frank X. Braun, "The Forty-Eighters in Politics," in Zucker, ed., *The Forty-Eighters,* pp. 137-41; Bergquist, p. 209.

57. See the "Biographical Dictionary of the Forty-Eighters," in Zucker, ed. *The Forty-Eighters,* pp. 269-357; Bruncken, p. 49.

58. Friedrich Kapp to Dr. Eduard Cohen, December 9, 1856, New York, Friedrich Kapp to Becker, September 6, 1852, New York, Friedrich Kapp Collection, Library of Congress; Frederick Law Olmsted to his father, January 22, 1855, Southside, Frederick Law Olmsted Collection, Library of Congress; Edith Lenel, *Friedrich Kapp* (Leipzig, 1935), p. 88; Zucker, ed., *The Forty-Eighters,* pp. 307-8; Roper, "Frederick Law Olmsted and the Western Texas Free-Soil Movement," *American Historical Review,* XVI, 60.

59. Friedrich Kapp to Frau Weydemeyer, April 18, 1866, New York, Joseph Weydemeyer Collection, Library of Congress; Kapp to Dr. Eduard Cohen, July 2, 1864, New York, Friedrich Kapp Collection, Library of Congress; Friedrich Kapp, *Geschichte der Deutschen im Staate New York* (New York, 1869), pp. 1-19; Lenel, pp. 76, 81-84; Friedrich Kapp, *Aus und Über Amerika* (Berlin, 1876), II, 48.

60. Kapp, *Aus und Über Amerika,* II, 26, 35, 88, 163.

61. Friedrich Kapp to Becker, January 2, 1857, New York, Friedrich Kapp Collection, Library of Congress; Lenel, pp. 48-49; Faust, II, 131-32; Zucker, ed. *The Forty-Eighters,* p. 308; "Friedrich Kapp," *Dictionary of American Biography,* X, 259-60.

62. Eugene H. Roseboom, *The Civil War Era, 1850-1873,* Vol. IV of *The History of the State of Ohio,* ed. Carl Wittke (Columbus, 1944), 213-19, 286-87.

63. Wittke, *Refugees of Revolution,* pp. 127-28, 136; Bruncken, p. 51; Thompson and Braun in Zucker, p. 118.

64. Timothy C. Day to Friedrich Hassaurek, March 11, 1856, Washington, Salmon P. Chase to Friedrich Hassaurek, April 7, 1857, Columbus, Friedrich Hassaurek Collection, Ohio State Historical Society.

65. Faust, II, 131; Carl Wittke, "Friedrich Hassaurek: Cincinnati's Leading Forty-Eighter," *The Ohio Historical Quarterly,* LXVIII (1959), 7; A. L. Chetlain to Friedrich Hassaurek, July 2, 1860, Galena, Illinois, A. H. Comier to Friedrich Hassaurek, September 26, 1860, Indianapolis, Friedrich Hassaurek Collection, Ohio State Historical Society; Wittke, *Against the Current,* pp. 121-22. Heinzen's later hatred for Hassaurek, despite their mutual republicanism and anticlericalism, probably resulted from their rivalry over leadership of the Cincinnati Germans during Heinzen's brief residence there in the fifties.

66. Timothy C. Day to Friedrich Hassaurek, June 24, 1856, March 11, 1856, Washington, John A. Gurley to Hassaurek, August 25, 1856, May 1, 1860, Washington, Friedrich Hassaurek Collection, Ohio State Historical Society; Zucker, ed. *The Forty-Eighters,* pp. 300-301; Roseboom, pp. 205, 371.

67. Wittke points out that Hassaurek became almost ultra-conservative on social and economic issues in his later years. See Carl Wittke, *The Ohio Historical Quarterly,* LXVIII, 13.

68. Carl Schurz to Adolf Meyer, April 18, 1852, London, in *Intimate Letters of Carl Schurz, 1841-1869,* ed. Joseph Schafer (Madison, 1928), pp. 107-11; Carl Schurz, *Reminiscences* (New York, 1907), I, 400; Claude Moore Fuess, *Carl Schurz, Reformer* (New York, 1963), pp. 1-40; Chester Verne Easum, *The Americanization of Carl Schurz* (Chicago, 1929), pp. 50-55.

69. Carl Schurz to Margarethe Schurz, March 23, 1854, Washington, Carl Schurz Collection, Library of Congress; Schurz, *Reminiscences,* II, 9, 28-29.

70. Schurz, *Reminiscences,* II, 49, 80-82; Carl Schurz to Abraham Lincoln, May 22, 1860, Watertown, Schurz to Mrs. Schurz, March 2, 1860, Milwaukee, in *Speeches, Correspondence and Political Papers of Carl Schurz,* ed. Fredrick Bancroft (New York, 1913), I, 116-18, 108; Fuess, pp. 57-59; Bayard Quincy Morgan, "Carl Schurz," in Zucker, ed., *The Forty-Eighters,* pp. 227, 232.

71. Carl Schurz to Gottfried Kinkel, February 15, 1858, Madison,

Wisconsin, in Schafer, pp. 182-84; Hawgood, p. 257; Zucker, ed. *The Forty-Eighters*, p. 341.

CHAPTER IV

1. United States Immigration Commission, *Report of the Immigration Commission: 1907-1910*, I, 63; Maldwyn A. Jones, *American Immigration* (Chicago, 1960), p. 208.

2. Issac Hourwich, *Immigration and Labor: The Economic Aspects of European Immigration to the United States* (New York, 1912), pp. 9-13; Jones, pp. 205-6, 4-5. Maldwyn Jones has labeled this terminology misleading and even distortive since immigrants, of whatever time and place, experience a process of adjustment. However, later immigrants underwent a more painful adjustment process due to the greater cultural gap that separated Eastern Europeans from Americans and also due to the more mature nature of American society at the time of their arrival. Historians should avoid beclouding significant differences in their zeal to erase labels born of the bias of those contemporary nativists who invented the terms.

3. Rudolph J. Vecoli, "Contadini in Chicago: a Critique of *The Uprooted*," *Journal of American History*, LI (December, 1964), 404-5; Stephen Thernstrom, *Poverty and Progress: Social Mobility in a Nineteenth Century City* (New York, 1969), p. 160.

4. Bernard A. Weisberger, *The New Industrial Society* (New York, 1969), pp. 12-17, 89, 7; Jones, p. 218.

5. Herbert Gutman remarks that "Too few workers belonged to trade unions to make them that important" to historians, who have, nevertheless, focused on them. See Herbert Gutman, "The Workers Search for Power: Labor in the Gilded Age," in *The Gilded Age: A Reappraisal*, ed. H. Wayne Morgan (Syracuse, 1963), p. 38.

6. Gerald N. Grob, *Workers and Utopia* (Chicago, 1969), pp. 7-8, 37-39, 133, 146-47. Norman Ware argues that in the fifties workers came to accept their status as permanent. See Norman Ware, *The Industrial Worker* (Chicago, 1964), p. 227. The founding fathers of American labor history, John R. Commons and Selig Perlman (the latter coined the term "job-conscious unionism"), limited their work to the organized labor movement. Only lately have historians transcended such exclusiveness.

7. Joseph G. Rayback, *A History of American Labor* (rev. ed.; New York, 1966), pp. 132-33. The most extensive and exhaustive treatment of the "Molly Maguire Riots" is to be found in Wayne G. Broehl, Jr., *The Molly Maguires* (Cambridge, Massachusetts, 1968).

8. Herbert G. Gutman, "Reconstruction in Ohio: Negroes in the

Hocking Valley Coal Mines in 1873 and 1874," *Labor History*, III (Fall, 1962), 243-47, 259; Gutman in Morgan, pp. 48-52; Edwin Fenton, "Italian Immigrants in the Stoneworkers' Union," *Labor History*, III (Spring, 1962), 188; Victor R. Greene, *The Slavic Community on Strike: Immigrant Labor in Pennsylvania Anthracite* (Notre Dame, 1968), p. 211; Louis Levine, *The Women's Garment Workers* (New York, 1969), p. 44.

9. David Brody, *Steelworkers in America: the Nonunion Era* (New York, 1969), p. 140; Greene, pp. 211-14.

10. J. Joseph Huthmacher, "Urban Liberalism and the Age of Reform," *Mississippi Valley Historical Review*, XLIX (September, 1962), 237-38.

11. Rowland Tappan Berthoff, *British Immigrants in Industrial America, 1790-1950* (Cambridge, Massachusetts, 1953), pp. 47-49, 54-55.

12. Berthoff, p. 49, 53; John Laslett, *Labor and the Left: a Study of Socialist and Radical Influences in the American Labor Movement, 1881-1924* (New York, 1970), pp. 193-95.

13. Berthoff, pp. 91-93.

14. Laslett, p. 199, 193-94; Berthoff, p. 55.

15. Berthoff, pp. 54-55; Laslett, pp. 205-13.

16. Robert Hunter to Adolph Germer, March 18, 1910, Adolph Germer to Robert Hunter, March 28, July 31, November 1, 1910, Germer to John H. Walker, February 7, 1913, Chicago, Adolph Germer Collection, State Historical Society of Wisconsin; *Miners' Magazine*, February, 1913. While there is no biography of Germer, his career can be traced in the collection of his papers and, among others, in the Morris Hillquit Collection at the State Historical Society of Wisconsin, the Victor Berger Collection at the Milwaukee County Historical Society, and the Eugene V. Debs Collection at Tamiment Institute, New York City.

17. Melvyn Dubofsky, *We Shall Be All: A History of the I.W.W.* (Chicago, 1969), pp. 23-26, 37, 56; Laslett, pp. 241-50.

18. Dubofsky, pp. 66-67; Laslett, p. 245; George C. Suggs, Jr., "Catalyst for Industrial Change: The W.F.M., 1893-1903," *Colorado Magazine*, XLV (1968), 333-36. There is no biography of Boyce, as in the case of Germer. His brief career in the labor movement can best be traced through conventions of the Federation, up to his retirement in 1902.

19. Laslett, pp. 253-57; Dubofsky, pp. 66-69. The lengthy quotation is from Boyce's address to the 1902 W.F.M. convention as excerpted in Laslett, p. 256.

20. Selig Perlman and Philip Taft, *Labor Movements, 1896-1932,*

Vol. IV of *History of Labour in the United States,* ed. John R. Commons (New York, 1935), 266-68.

21. William M. Leiserson, *Adjusting Immigrant and Industry* (New York, 1924), p. 178; Dubofsky, pp. 148-54, 161-65.

22. Information on such I.W.W. activists is scarce. The best, although tedious, way to trace their careers is through perusal of Wobbly publications, the *Industrial Worker* and the *Industrial Union Bulletin,* or other contemporary radical journals, such as the *International Socialist Review.* Dubofsky's book on the I.W.W. presents some gleanings. Only lately have scholarly studies of such secondary Wobbly leaders been undertaken. See, for example, Kara P. Brewer, "The American Career of James Connolly" (unpublished M.A. thesis, University of the Pacific, 1972).

23. Donald B. Cole, *Immigrant City: Lawrence, Massachusetts, 1845-1921* (Chapel Hill, North Carolina, 1963), pp. 68-75, 120-21.

24. *Ibid.*, p. 179, 193; Dubofsky, p. 241, 250, 257-58; Perlman and Taft, p. 273; Paul F. Brissenden, *The I.W.W.: A Study of American Syndicalism* (New York, 1919), p. 290. Brissenden refers to the Lawrence strike as more of a social revolution than a strike.

25. Dubofsky, pp. 270-81.

26. J. M. Budish and George Soule, *The New Unionism in the Clothing Industry* (New York, 1920), p. 49; Levine, pp. 12-19; Laslett, pp. 101-2.

27. Levine, pp. 24-31; Laslett, pp. 99-101, 117; Melvyn Dubofsky, *When Workers Organize: New York City in the Progressive Era* (Amherst, 1968), pp. 16-18; Budish and Soule, pp. 49-60. Moses Rischin, *The Promised City: New York's Jews, 1870-1914* (New York, 1970), p. 193 argues that ". . . traits that [at first] made Jewish workmen reluctant union members would make them able labor leaders and rank and filers in humanly complex and morselized industries. A study of workmen's leisure habits revealed that [they] led all other nationalities in club and lodge activity and stood first in night school and public lecture attendance. . . ."

28. Levine, p. 85, 103; Benjamin Stolberg, *Tailor's Progress: The Story of a Famous Union and the Men Who Made It* (New York, 1944), pp. 47-49; Rischin, pp. 181-82.

29. Rischin, p. 247, 250-52; Laslett, p. 109.

30. Charles H. Winslow, "Conciliation, Arbitration, and Sanitation in the Cloak, Suit, and Skirt Industry in New York City," U. S. Bureau of Labor Statistics, *Bulletin,* IIC (January, 1912), 211-17; Rischin, p. 252; Laslett, p. 109. For a history of the Amalgamated, see Charles Elbert Zaretz, *The Amalgamated Clothing Workers of America: A Study in Progressive Trade Unionism* (New York, 1934).

31. No biography of Schlesinger exists. His life in outline is found

in Solon DeLeon, ed., *American Labor Who's Who* (New York, 1925), pp. 205-6, and in *Dictionary of American Biography*, XVI, 1935, 436-37. He appears in secondary studies of the garment unions and in union proceedings and publications.

32. "Benjamin Schlesinger," *Dictionary of American Biography*, XVI, 436-37; Levine, pp. 93, 109, 115, 467, 474, 484, 487; Dubofsky, *When Workers Organize*, p. 62.

33. For biographical data, see the unsigned typescript biography in Box D50, Meyer London Collection, Tamiment Institute, New York City. A highly romanticized version of his life is found in Harry Rogoff, *An East Side Epic: The Life and Work of Meyer London* (New York, 1930).

34. "Meyer London," *Dictionary of American Biography*, XI (1933), 372-74; Dubofsky, *When Workers Organize*, pp. 64-66.

35. "Work of Meyer London in the Sixty-Fourth Congress," *American Labor Year Book*, 1916, I, 102-3; "Meyer London Congressional Resolutions," Box 49D, Meyer London Collection, Tamiment Institute; Rogoff, p. 196.

36. After the First World War, a number of the immigrant union leaders became national figures and even presidential advisers. Two men who came to attain such stature were David Dubinsky (1892-19–) of the I.L.G.W.U. and Sidney Hillman (1887-1946) of the A.C.W.

37. Laslett, p. 103, 117-23, 231; Budish and Soule, p. 172, 193-95, 203-4. The involvement of these unions in the lives of their members is reminiscent of the powerful German Social Democratic party and its enveloping of its members in pre-World War I Germany.

38. Laslett, p. 126.

CHAPTER V

1. Henry David, *The History of the Haymarket Affair: A Study in the American Social-Revolutionary and Labor Movements* (New York, 1963), p. 88.

2. Morris Hillquit, *History of Socialism in the United States* (New York, 1910), p. 177.

3. Howard H. Quint, *The Forging of American Socialism: Origins of the Modern Movement* (Indianapolis, 1964), p. 8; Daniel Bell, *Marxian Socialism in the United States* (Princeton, 1967), p. 21.

4. David Herreschoff, *American Disciples of Marx: From the Age of Jackson to the Progressive Era* (Detroit, 1967), pp. 56-59, 68; John R. Commons, *History of Labour in the United States* (New York, 1918), II, 207; Hermann Schlüter, *Die Internationale in Amerika* (Chicago, 1918), p. 85.

5. Commons, II, 207. Bakunin's anarchism is briefly considered below.

6. Schlüter, *Die Internationale in Amerika*, pp. 80-81, 86-87; Herreshoff, pp. 74-7; Commons, II, 207-8.

7. John R. Commons, ed., *A Documentary History of American Industrial Society* (Cleveland, 1911), IX, 358; Schlüter, *Die Internationale in Amerika*, pp. 293-94; Commons, *History of Labour . . .* , II, 216-19; Hillquit, p. 179; Quint, p. 9-11.

8. Friedrich A. Sorge, "Socialism and the Worker," in *Socialism in America from the Shakers to the Third International, a Documentary History*, ed. Albert Fried (New York, 1970), pp. 198-207; Herreshoff, p. 94, 100-103; Commons, *History of Labour . . .* , II, 222.

9. See the quotation from V. L. Rosenberg, party secretary, in Charles Madison, *Critics and Crusaders* (second ed.; New York, 1959), p. 450.

10. Quint, pp. 25, 35, 60; Commons, *History of Labour . . .* , II, 514-17.

11. Quint, pp. 142-46; Madison, pp. 450-51, 470-75.

12. Daniel DeLeon, "Reform or Revolution," in Fried, pp. 244-46, 254-55. For DeLeon's most damning appraisal of socialists in public office, see his series blasting the first socialist elected to the United States Congress: "Berger's Hits and Misses," *Daily People*, April to October, 1911.

13. Quint, p. 168; Herreshoff, p. 148.

14. Quint, pp. 161-67; Herreshoff, pp. 120-21.

15. Quint, p. 174; Nathan Fine, *Labor and Farmer Parties in the United States, 1828-1928* (New York, 1928), p. 88; Ira Kipnis, *The American Socialist Movement, 1897-1912* (New York, 1952), p. 19. A balanced and comprehensive biography of DeLeon is still lacking. Those available are from the pens of disciples. See especially Arnold Peterson, *Daniel DeLeon: Social Architect* (New York, 1941). For a revisionist review of DeLeon's career, see Don K. McKee, "Daniel DeLeon: A Reappraisal," *Labor History*, I (Fall, 1960), 264-97.

16. Hillquit, pp. 294-304; Quint, pp. 292-95.

17. Hillquit, pp. 308-9; Kipnis, p. 104; Quint, p. 388.

18. See the several appendices to Socialist Party, *Proceedings* of the 1912 National Convention. This document, often reprinted and readily accessible, clearly reveals major positions upheld by the party between 1901 and 1917.

19. Sally M. Miller, *Victor Berger and the Promise of Constructive Socialism, 1910-1920* (Westport, Connecticut, 1973), pp. 17-18, 22-33; Marvin Wachman, *History of the Social-Democratic Party of Milwaukee, 1897-1910* (Urbana, 1945), pp. 9-19; Edward J. Muzik,

"Victor L. Berger, a Biography" (unpublished Ph.D. Dissertation, Northwestern University, 1960), pp. 17-69.

20. *Social-Democratic Herald,* June 7, 1913.

21. *Ibid.,* April 5, 1905.

22. Socialist Party, *Proceedings* of the 1908 National Convention, pp. 143-44; Victor Berger to Morris Hillquit, April 8, 1905, Milwaukee, Morris Hillquit Collection, State Historical Society of Wisconsin; Berger as quoted in Lincoln Steffens, "Eugene V. Debs on What the Matter Is in America and What to Do About It," *Everybody's,* XIX (October, 1908), 461.

23. *Social Democratic Herald,* April 9, 1910; David A. Shannon, *The Socialist Party of America* (Chicago, 1967), pp. 21-25.

24. Socialist Party, *Proceedings* of the 1912 National Convention, pp. 233-36; Roderick Nash, "Victor Berger: Making Marx Respectable," *Wisconsin Magazine of History,* XLVII (Summer, 1964), 307-8; Sally M. Miller, "A Socialist Represents Milwaukee," *Historical Messenger* (Milwaukee), XXII (December, 1966), 132-38.

25. A lively historiographical argument exists over the peaking of the Socialist party in 1912. Daniel Bell maintains that the party declined thereafter, David Shannon does not see growth beyond that date, and James Weinstein in *The Decline of Socialism in America, 1912-1925* (New York, 1967) claims that the party maintained its vigor into the war years.

26. Shannon, pp. 10-11; Morris Hillquit, *Loose Leaves from a Busy Life* (New York, 1934), pp. 18-29.

27. Morris Hillquit–William D. Haywood Debate, "Socialist Tactics," 1911, New York, typescript in Box 8, Morris Hillquit Collection, State Historical Society of Wisconsin; Morris Hillquit, *Socialism in Theory and Practice* (New York, 1912), p. 162. Morris Hillquit to J. G. Phelps Stokes, December 3, 1909, New York, Hillquit Collection, State Historical Society of Wisconsin; Hillquit to Julius Gerber, May 18, 1914, New York, Morris Hillquit Collection, Tamiment Institute.

28. Morris Hillquit–William D. Haywood Debate, "What Shall the Attitude of the Socialist Party Be Toward the Economic Organization of the Workers," 1912, New York, typescript in Morris Hillquit Collection, Tamiment Institute; Hillquit, *Loose Leaves from a Busy Life,* pp. 99-100.

29. Moses Rischin, *The Promised City* (New York, 1970), p. 234; Shannon, pp. 104-5.

30. The only biographical works on Hillquit are Robert William Iverson, "Morris Hillquit: American Social Democrat" (unpublished Ph.D. Dissertation, State University of Iowa, 1951), and a manuscript by his daughter, Nina Hillquit, "Morris Hillquit, Pioneer of

American Socialism," Morris Hillquit Collection, Box 12, State Historical Society of Wisconsin.

31. See Socialist Party, *Proceedings* of the 1917 Emergency Convention (2 vols.).

32. Edward J. Muzik, "Victor L. Berger: Congress and the Red Scare," *Wisconsin Magazine of History*, XLVII (Summer, 1964), 309-18; Robert K. Murray, *Red Scare: A Study in National Hysteria, 1919-1920* (New York, 1964), 242-44.

33. For party concern over the growing alien tones of some members, see Adolph Germer to Morris Hillquit, April 17, 1919, Chicago, Morris Hillquit Collection, State Historical Society of Wisconsin.

34. Esther Corey, "Lewis Corey (Louis C. Fraina), 1892-1953: A Bibliography with Autobiographical Notes," *Labor History*, IV (Spring, 1963), 109, 112.

35. *Ibid.*, 105-6; Theodore Draper, *The Roots of American Communism* (New York, 1963), pp. 62-64; *New Review*, III (February, 1915), 138.

36. *New Review*, IV (April, 1916), 103-4; *Class Struggle*, May, 1919, p. 227; *The Revolutionary Age*, December 18, 1918, p. 2, February 8, 1919, pp. 4-6; Louis C. Fraina, *Revolutionary Socialism*, in Fried, pp. 530-38.

37. Shannon, pp. 131-49.

38. James Joll, *The Anarchists* (New York, 1964), p. 12.

39. G. D. H. Cole, *Marxism and Anarchism, 1850-1890*, Vol. II of *A History of Socialist Thought* (London, 1964), 337-40; Joll analyzes the evolution of anarchist theory. Individualistic anarchism, such as that associated with Thoreau and Benjamin Tucker is excluded from this discussion; see Joll, pp. 17-58.

40. Cole, II, 353.

41. Joll, pp. 128-29, 138.

42. David, p. 32, 87-100; Commons, *History of Labour . . .*, II, 390-91.

43. David, p. 91, 123-27. Probably disagreement existed over the value of the trade union as the basis of the new society.

44. *Ibid.*, pp. 148-50; *Alarm*, December 12, 1885, March 30, 1886.

45. David, pp. 156, 436; Joll, 142-43; Henry Pelling, *American Labor* (Chicago, 1960), pp. 71-72; Quint, p. 33.

46. August Vincent Spies, "Autobiographical Sketch," pp. 17-18, 23-24, 26-27, 29-30, Haymarket Square Riot Collection, Chicago Historical Society. The autobiographical sketches of the eight defendants have been collected and are found in Philip S. Foner, ed., *The Autobiographies of the Haymarket Martyrs* (New York, 1969).

47. Leon Stein and Philip Taft, eds., *The Accused and the Ac-*

cusers: The Famous Speeches of the Eight Chicago Anarchists in Court (New York, 1970), pp. 5-18; *Alarm,* November 19, 1887.

48. David, pp. 439-40; Joll, pp. 139-41.

49. David, p. 85; Joll, p. 141.

50. Commons, *History of Labour . . . ,* II, 293-94. For the only biography of Most, see Rudolf Rocker, *Johann Most: Das Leben eines Rebellen* (Berlin, 1924).

51. *Freiheit,* May 21, 1904; Rocker, pp. 154-55.

52. John Most, *The Beast of Property* (New Haven, n.d.), pp. 9-12; John Most, *The God Pestilance* [*sic*] (New York, n.d.), pp. 17-18.

53. Most, *Beast of Property,* pp. 11-2; Rocker, p. 7.

54. Rocker, pp. 6-7.

55. The early years of each can be traced in Emma Goldman, *Living My Life* (New York, 1931) and in Alexander Berkman, *Prison Memoirs of an Anarchist* (New York, 1912).

56. Johann Most condemned Berkman's act, partially because of his jealousy over Goldman, it appears; this incident served to release Emma Goldman from her worshipful regard for Most. Goldman, I, 85-87, 96-98; Berkman, pp. 4-5.

57. Richard Drinnon, *Rebel in Paradise: A Biography of Emma Goldman* (Boston, 1961), pp. 81-82, "The Psychology of Political Violence," in *Anarchism and Other Essays* (New York, 1917), pp. 98-99, 113. In 1908, the federal government revoked the naturalization papers of Emma Goldman's former husband, thereby denaturalizing her and paving the way for her later expulsion from the United States.

58. *Mother Earth,* November, 1907, p. 378, December, 1908, p. 353, July, 1910, p. 163; Drinnon, p. 63.

59. For a glimpse of Berkman as a private person, see Emma Goldman to Agnes Inglis, Cleveland, February 5, 1917, M. Eleanor Fitzgerald to Agnes Inglis, New York, July 12, 1917, Emma Goldman Papers, Joseph Labadie Collection, University of Michigan. Berkman, *Prison Memoirs of an Anarchist,* p. 9; *The Blast,* January 1, 1917, p. 2; Alexander Berkman to Joseph Labadie, March 18, 1916, San Francisco, Alexander Berkman Papers, Joseph Labadie Collection, University of Michigan.

60. *Mother Earth,* June, 1907, p. 179, October, 1907, p. 310, October, 1910, p. 244.

61. *Ibid.,* March, 1907, pp. 6-7, February, 1910, pp. 385-87; *The Blast,* December 15, 1916, p. 4;. Emma Goldman to Agnes Inglis, November 16, 1916, Chicago, Emma Goldman Papers, Joseph Labadie Collection, University of Michigan.

62. *Mother Earth,* April, 1912, p. 45, February, 1913, p. 417, May, 1907, pp. 127-28, October, 1907, p. 316; Emma Goldman,

"Anarchism: What It Really Stands For," in *Anarchism and Other Essays*, p. 73.

63. *Mother Earth*, January, 1913, pp. 373-77.

64. *Ibid.*, December, 1910, pp. 326-27, November, 1907, pp. 387-88; Emma Goldman to Agnes Inglis, May 3, 1917, New York, June 20, 1917, New York, Emma Goldman Papers, Joseph Labadie Collection, University of Michigan.

65. Goldman, "Anarchism: What It Really Stands For," in *Anarchism and Other Essays*, pp. 56-59, 64-68.

66. Emma Goldman to Agnes Inglis, February 5, 1917, Cleveland, April 4, 1917, Philadelphia, Emma Goldman Papers, Joseph Labadie Collection, University of Michigan.

67. *The Blast*, March 15, 1917, p. 3; Alexander Berkman to Joseph Labadie, March 18, 1916, San Francisco, February 2, 1917, San Francisco, Alexander Berkman Papers, Joseph Labadie Collection, University of Michigan; Emma Goldman to Agnes Inglis, July 30, 1917, Jefferson City Penitentiary, Emma Goldman Papers, Joseph Labadie Collection, University of Michigan.

68. Alexander Berkman, "Russian Diary of 1920-1922," January 4, 1920, p. 8. Emma Goldman Collection, New York Public Library; Emma Goldman to Bayard Boyesen, February 20, 1923, Germany, Emma Goldman Collection, New York Public Library.

69. Drinnon, pp. 109-11.

Chapter VI

1. This figure is reached by computing the ages of all personalities focused upon, excluding Etienne Cabet whose immigration at age sixty represents a distinctive path that precludes inclusion.

2. Kenneth Keniston, *Young Radicals: Notes on Committed Youth* (New York, 1968), pp. 326-30. This study of student radicals of the sixties in the United States offers insights useful to understanding the alienated radicals of the past.

3. *Ibid.*, p. 340.

4. R. Laurence Moore, *European Socialists and the American Promised Land* (New York, 1970), pp. 33-34, 41-46, 101. Moore provides a good summary of the convolutions the Marxist evaluation of the United States underwent.

5. David Caute, *The Left in Europe Since 1789* (New York, 1966), p. 30.

Selected Bibliography

MANUSCRIPT COLLECTIONS

Fritz Anneke and Mathilde Franziska Giesler-Anneke Papers. State Historical Society of Wisconsin.
Victor L. Berger Collection. Milwaukee County Historical Society.
Alexander Berkman Papers, Joseph A. Labadie Collection. University of Michigan.
Eugene V. Debs Collection. Tamiment Institute. New York City.
Ferdinand J. Dreer Collection. Historical Society of Pennsylvania.
George Flower Collection. Chicago Historical Society.
Edward Carey Gardiner Collection. Historical Society of Pennsylvania.
Albert Gallatin Collection. New York Historical Society.
Adolph Germer Collection. State Historical Society of Wisconsin.
Emma Goldman Collection. New York Public Library.
Emma Goldman Papers, Joseph A. Labadie Collection. University of Michigan.
Friedrich Hassaurek Collection. The Ohio State Historical Society.
Haymarket Square Riot Collection. Chicago Historical Society.
Morris Hillquit Collection. State Historical Society of Wisconsin.
Morris Hillquit Collection. Tamiment Institute. New York City.
Friedrich Kapp Collection. Library of Congress.
Eben Lane Collection. Chicago Historical Society.
Meyer London Collection. Tamiment Institute. New York City.
Frederick Law Olmsted Collection. Library of Congress.
Robert Dale Owen Collection. Indiana State Library.
Robert Dale Owen Papers. Indiana Historical Society.
Robert Owen Papers. Library Co-operative Union Ltd. Manchester, England.
Ernestine Rose Collection. Vassar College.
George A. Schilling Collection. University of Chicago.
Carl Schurz Collection. Library of Congress.
Wilhelm Weitling Collection. New York Public Library.
Joseph Weydemeyer Collection. Library of Congress.
Frances Wright Papers. Library of Congress.

NEWSPAPERS AND PERIODICALS

Alarm, 1884-1888.
Atlantische Studien von Deutschen in Amerika, 1853-1854.

The Blast, 1916-1917.
Class Struggle, 1917-1919.
Daily Sentinel, 1830.
Die Republik der Arbeiter, 1850-1851.
Free Enquirer, 1828-1834.
Freiheit, 1902-1904.
Industrial Union Bulletin, 1907-1909.
Internationalist Socialist Review, 1900-1917.
Man, 1834.
Mother Earth, 1906-1917.
New Harmony Gazette, 1825-1828.
New Review, 1913-1916.
New York Evening Post, 1829-1830.
Radical Reformer and Working Man's Advocate, 1835.
The Revolutionary Age, 1918-1919.
Social Democratic Herald, 1897-1913.
Turn-Zeitung, 1852.
Weekly People, 1891-1900.
Working Man's Advocate, 1829-1830; 1842; 1844-1845.

GOVERNMENT DOCUMENTS, PROCEEDINGS, AND YEAR BOOKS

American Labor Year Book. 1916.
DeLeon, Solon, ed. *American Labor Who's Who.* New York, 1925.
Dictionary of American Biography.
Socialist Party. *Proceedings* of the National Conventions, 1901-1917.
United States. Commission on Immigration. *Report of the Immigration Commission,* 1907-1910.

PRIMARY WORKS

BANCROFT, FREDRICK, ed. *Speeches, Correspondence and Political Papers of Carl Schurz.* New York, 1913.
BERKMAN, ALEXANDER. *Prison Memoirs of an Anarchist.* New York, 1912.
BROTHERS, THOMAS. *The United States of North America As They Are; Not As They Are Generally Described; Being a Cure For Radicalism.* London, 1840.
BYRDSALL, F. *The History of the Loco-Foco or Equal Rights Party: Its Movements, Conventions, and Proceedings With Short Characteristic Sketches of Its Prominent Men.* New York, 1867.
COREY, ESTHER. "Lewis Corey (Louis C. Fraina), 1892-1953: A Bibliography with Autobiographical Notes." *Labor History,* IV (Spring, 1963), 103-31.

"Diary of William Owen From November 10, 1824 to April 20, 1825." Ed. Joel W. Hiatt. *Indiana Historical Society Publications,* Vol. IV. Indianapolis, 1906.

DOUAI, ADOLF. *Land und Leute in der Union.* Berlin, 1864.

EVANS, FREDERICK WILLIAM. *Autobiography of a Shaker.* New York, 1869.

FONER, PHILIP S., ed. *The Autobiographies of the Haymarket Martyrs.* New York, 1969.

FRIED, ALBERT, ed. *Socialism in America: From the Shakers to the Third International. A Documentary History.* New York, 1970.

GILBERT, AMOS. *Memoir of Frances Wright: The Pioneer Woman in the Cause of Human Rights.* Cincinnati, 1855.

GOLDMAN, EMMA. *Living My Life.* 2 volumes. New York, 1931.

————. "The Psychology of Political Violence." *Anarchism and Other Essays.* New York, 1917.

HEIGHTON, WILLIAM. "The Principles of Aristocratic Legislation, Developed in an Address delivered to the Working People of the District of Southmark, and Township of Moyamensing and Passyunk." August 14, 1828. Philadelphia, 1828.

HEINZEN, KARL. *Erlebtes Zweiter Theil: Nach Meiner Exilirung.* Boston, 1874.

————. *Murder and Liberty.* Indianapolis, 1881.

————. *The Rights of Women and the Sexual Relations.* Chicago, 1891.

————. *Teutscher Radikalismus in Amerika.* Boston, 1867.

————. *What Is Humanity?* Indianapolis, 1877.

————. *What Is Real Democracy?* Indianapolis, 1871.

HILLQUIT, MORRIS. *History of Socialism in the United States.* New York, 1910.

————. *Loose Leaves From a Busy Life.* New York, 1934.

————. *Socialism in Theory and Practice.* New York, 1912.

JONES, MARY HARRIS. *Autobiography of Mother Jones.* Chicago, 1925.

KAPP, FRIEDRICH. *Aus und Über Amerika.* Berlin, 1876.

————. *Geschichte der Deutschen im Staate New York.* New York, 1869.

KOERNER, GUSTAVE. *Memoirs of Gustave Koerner, 1809-1896.* 2 vols. Cedar Rapids, Iowa, 1909.

KRADITOR, AILEEN S., ed. *Up From the Pedestal: Selected Writings in the History of American Feminism.* Chicago, 1968.

MACLURE, WILLIAM. *Opinions on Various Subjects, Dedicated to the Industrious Producers.* 3 vols. New Harmony, 1831.

MARTINEAU, HARRIET. *Society in America.* London, 1837.

MASQUERIER, LEWIS. *Sociology: or the Reconstruction of Society, Government and Property.* New York, 1877.

MITCHELL, JOHN. *Organized Labor*. Philadelphia, 1903.

MOST, JOHN. *The Beast of Property*. New Haven, n.d.

—————. *The God Pestilence* [*sic*]. New York, n.d.

NEVINS, ALLEN, ed. *Diary of Philip Hone*. 2 vols. New York, 1927.

OLMSTED, FREDERICK LAW. *Journey Through Texas: A Saddle-Trip on the Southwestern Frontier*. Ed. James Howard. Austin, 1962.

OWEN, ROBERT DALE. *To Holland and to New Harmony: Robert Dale Owen's Travel Journal, 1825-1826*. Ed. Josephine M. Elliott. Indiana Historical Society Publications, Vol. XXIII. Indianapolis, 1969.

—————. *Threading My Way*. New York, 1874.

OWEN, ROBERT DALE and FRANCES WRIGHT. *Tracts on Republican Government and National Education Addressed to the Inhabitants of the United States of America*. London, 1851.

POESCHE, THEODORE and CHARLES GROEPP. *The New Rome: or the United States of the World*. New York, 1853.

SCHAFER, JOSEPH, ed. *Intimate Letters of Carl Schurz, 1841-1869*. Madison, 1928.

SCHURZ, CARL. *Reminiscences*. 3 vols. New York, 1907.

SORGE, FRIEDRICH A. "Joseph Weydemeyer und sein Antheil an der deutschen Bewegung der vierziger Jahre und an der Amerikanischen Bewegung der funfziger Jahre." *Pionier*, 1897, 54-60.

STANTON, ELIZABETH C., SUSAN B. ANTHONY, and MATILDA GAGE, *History of Woman Suffrage*. 6 vols. New York, 1881-1922.

STEFFENS, LINCOLN. "Eugene V. Debs on What the Matter Is in America and What to Do About It." *Everybody's*, XIX (October, 1908), 455-69.

STEIN, LEON and PHILIP TAFT, eds. *The Accused and the Accusers: The Famous Speeches of the Eight Chicago Anarchists in Court*. New York, 1970.

SYLVESTER, LORNA LUTES, ed. "Miner K. Kellogg: Recollections of New Harmony." *Indiana Magazine of History*, LXIV (March, 1968), 39-64.

TROLLOPE, FRANCES. *Domestic Manners of the Americans*. Ed. Donald Smalley. New York, 1949.

UNDERWOOD, SARA A. *Heroines of Free Thought*. New York, 1876.

WINSLOW, CHARLES H. "Conciliation, Arbitration and Sanitation in the Cloak, Suit, and Skirt Industry in New York City." *Bulletin*, United States Bureau of Labor Statistics. IIC (January, 1912).

WRIGHT, FRANCES. *Biography and Notes of*. New York, 1844.

—————. *Course of Popular Lectures*. Sixth edition. New York, 1836.

—————. *Views of Society and Manners in America*. Ed. Paul R. Baker. Cambridge, Massachusetts, 1963.

Selected Bibliography [199]

SECONDARY WORKS

ANDER, O. FRITIOF, ed. *In the Trek of the Immigrants: Essays Presented to Carl Wittke.* Rock Island, Illinois, 1964.

ARKY, LOUIS H. "The Mechanics' Union of Trade Associations and the Formation of the Philadelphia Workingmen's Movement." *Pennsylvania Magazine of History and Biography,* LXXI (April, 1952), 142-76.

BELL, DANIEL. *Marxian Socialism in the United States.* Princeton, 1967.

BERTHOFF, ROWLAND TAPPAN. *British Immigrants in Industrial America, 1790-1950.* Cambridge, Massachusetts, 1953.

BESTOR, ARTHUR E. "Albert Brisbane—Propagandist for Socialism in the 1840's." *New York History,* XXVIII (April, 1947), 128-58.

————. *Backwoods Utopias: the Sectarian and Owenite Phases of Communitarian Socialism in America, 1663-1829.* Philadelphia, 1950.

BIESELE, RUDOLPH LEOPOLD. *The History of the German Settlements in Texas, 1831-1861.* Austin, 1930.

————. "The Texas State Convention of Germans in 1854." *Southwestern Historical Quarterly,* XXXIII (April, 1930), 247-61.

BLAU, JOSEPH L. *Social Theories of Jacksonian Democracy.* New York, 1947.

BLOS, ANNA. *Frauen der deutschen Revolution, 1848.* Dresden, 1928.

BRISSENDEN, PAUL F. *The I.W.W.: A Study of American Syndicalism.* New York, 1920.

BRODY, DAVID. *Steelworkers in America: The Nonunion Era.* New York, 1969.

BROEHL, WAYNE G., JR. *The Molly Maguires.* Cambridge, Massachusetts, 1968.

BROWN, ANNA B. A. "A Dream of Emancipation." *New England Magazine,* XXX (June, 1904), 494-99.

BRUNCKEN, ERNEST. *German Political Refugees in the United States During the Period From 1815-1860.* 1904.

BUDISH, J. M. and GEORGE SOULE. *The New Unionism in the Clothing Industry.* New York, 1920.

CARTER, HARVEY L. "William Maclure." *Indiana Magazine of History,* XXXI (June, 1935), 83-91.

CLARK, FREDERICK C. "A Neglected Socialist." *Annals of the American Academy of Political and Social Science,* V. (1895), 66-87.

COLE, DONALD B. *Immigrant City: Lawrence, Massachusetts, 1845-1921.* Chapel Hill, North Carolina, 1963.

COLE, G. D. H. *The Forerunners.* Vol. I. *Marxism and Anarchism,*

1850-1890. Vol. II. *A History of Socialist Thought.* New York, 1965.

COMMONS, JOHN R., ed. *A Documentary History of American Industrial Society.* Ten volumes. Cleveland, 1911.

――――. *History of Labour in the United States.* Four volumes. New York, 1918-1935.

CAUTE, DAVID. *The Left in Europe Since 1789.* New York, 1966.

CUNZ, DIETER. "The Baltimore Germans and the Year 1848." *The American German Review,* X (1943), 30-33.

――――. "Carl Heinrich Schnauffers Literarische Versuche." *Publications of the Modern Language Association of America,* LIX (June, 1944), 524-39.

――――. *The Maryland Germans: A History.* New York, 1948.

DAVID, HENRY. *The History of the Haymarket Affair: A Study in the American Social-Revolutionary and Labor Movements.* New York, 1963.

――――. "Upheaval at Homestead." *America In Crisis.* Ed. Daniel Aaron. New York, 1952.

DRAPER, THEODORE. *The Roots of American Communism.* New York, 1963.

DRINNON, RICHARD. *Rebel in Paradise: A Biography of Emma Goldman.* Boston, 1961.

DUBOFSKY, MELVYN. *We Shall Be All: A History of the I.W.W., the Industrial Workers of the World.* Chicago, 1969.

――――. *When Workers Organize: New York City in the Progressive Era.* Amherst, 1968.

EASUM, CHESTER VERNE. *The Americanization of Carl Schurz.* Chicago, 1929.

EDINGER, DORA. "A Feminist Forty-eighter." *The American German Review,* XXXVIII (June, 1942), 18-20.

EMERSON, O. B. "Frances Wright and Her Nashoba Experiment." *Tennessee Historical Quarterly,* VI (1947), 291-314.

ERNST, ROBERT. *Immigrant Life in New York City, 1825-1863.* New York, 1959.

FAUST, ALBERT BERNHARDT. *The German Element in the United States with Special Reference to Its Political, Moral, Social and Educational Influence.* Boston, 1909.

――――. "Mathilde Franziska Giesler-Anneke: 'Memorien einer frau aus dem badishpfalzischer feldzug,' and a sketch of her career." *German-American Annals,* XVI (May-August, 1918), 73-140.

FENTON, EDWIN. "Italian Immigrants in the Stoneworker's Union." *Labor History,* III (Spring, 1962), 188-207.

FINE, NATHAN. *Labor and Farmer Parties in the United States, 1828-1928.* New York, 1928.

FUESS, CLAUDE MOORE. *Carl Cchurz, Reformer (1829-1906)*. New York, 1963.

GREENE, VICTOR R. *The Slavic Community on Strike: Immigrant Labor in Pennsylvania Anthracite*. Notre Dame, 1968.

GROB, GERALD N. *Workers and Utopia: A Study of Ideological Conflict in the American Labor Movement, 1865-1900*. Chicago, 1969.

GUTMAN, HERBERT G. "Reconstruction in Ohio: Negroes in the Hecking Valley Coal Mines in 1873 and 1874." *Labor History*, III (Fall, 1962), 243-64.

——————. "The Worker's Search For Power: Labor in the Gilded Age." *The Gilded Age: A Reappraisal*. Ed. H. Wayne Morgan. Syracuse, 1963.

HAMEROW, THEODORE S. *Restoration, Revolution, Reaction: Economics and Politics in Germany, 1816-1871*. Princeton, 1967.

HANDLIN, OSCAR. *The Uprooted: The Epic Story of the Great Migrations That Made the American People*. New York, 1951.

HANSEN, MARCUS L. "The Revolutions of 1848 and German Emigration." *Journal of Economic and Business History*, II (1930), 630-58.

HARRISON, JOHN F. C. *Quest for the New Moral World: Robert Owen and the Owenites in Britain and America*. New York, 1969.

HAWGOOD, JOHN. *The Tragedy of German-America: The Germans in the United States of America During the Nineteenth Century— And After*. New York, 1940.

HERRESHOFF, DAVID. *American Disciples of Marx: From the Age of Jackson to the Progressive Era*. Detroit, 1967.

HERRIOTT, F. I. "The Conference in the Deutsches Haus, Chicago, May 14-15, 1860: A Study of Some of the Preliminaries of the National Republican Convention of 1860." *Transactions of the Illinois State Historical Society*, XXXV (1928), 101-91.

HIGHAM, JOHN. *Strangers in the Land: Patterns of American Nativism, 1860-1925*. New York, 1955.

HILLQUIT, NINA. "Morris Hillquit, Pioneer of American Socialism." Morris Hillquit Collection. Wisconsin State Historical Socety.

HOBSBAWM, ERIC. *Primitive Rebels*. New York, 1965.

HOLLOWAY, MARK. *Heavens on Earth: Utopian Communities In America, 1680-1880*. New York, 1966.

HUGINS, WALTER. *Jacksonian Democracy and the Working Class: A Study of the New York Workingmen's Movement, 1829-1837*. Stanford, 1960.

HUTHMACHER, JOSEPH. "Urban Liberalism and the Age of Reform." *Mississippi Valley Historical Review*, XLIX (September, 1962).

JOLL, JAMES. *The Anarchists*. New York, 1964.

JONES, MALDWYN A. *American Immigration.* Chicago, 1960.

JOSEPH, SAMUEL. *Jewish Immigration to the United States.* New York, 1914.

KENISTON, KENNETH. *Young Radicals: Notes on Committed Youth.* New York, 1968.

KIPNIS, IRA. *The American Socialist Movement, 1897-1912.* New York, 1952.

LANE, MARGARET. *Frances Wright and the 'Great Experiment.'* Manchester, 1972.

LASLETT, JOHN. *Labor and Left: A Study of Socialist and Radical Influences in the American Labor Movement, 1881-1924.* New York, 1970.

LEISERSON, WILLIAM M. *Adjusting Immigrant and Industry.* New York, 1924.

LENEL, EDITH. *Friedrich Kapp.* Leipzig, 1935.

LEOPOLD, RICHARD W. *Robert Dale Owen: A Biography.* Cambridge, Massachusetts, 1940.

LEVINE, LOUIS. *The Women's Garment Workers.* New York, 1969.

LOCKWOOD, GEORGE B. *The New Harmony Movement.* New York, 1971.

LUEBKE, FREDERICK C., ed. *Ethnic Voters and the Election of Lincoln.* Lincoln, Nebraska, 1971.

MADISON, CHARLES. *Critics and Crusaders.* New York, 1959.

McKEE, DON K. "Daniel DeLeon: A Reappraisal." *Labor History,* I (Fall, 1960), 264-97.

MILLER, SALLY M. "A Socialist Represents Milwaukee." *Historical Messenger* (Milwaukee), XXII (December, 1966), 132-38.

—————. *Victor Berger and the Promise of Constructive Socialism, 1910-1920.* Westport, Connecticut, 1972.

MOORE, R. LAURENCE. *European Socialists and the American Promised Land.* New York, 1970.

MURRAY, ROBERT K. *Red Scare: A Study in National Hysteria, 1919-1920.* New York, 1964.

MUZIK, EDWARD J. "Victor L. Berger: Congress and the Red Scare." *Wisconsin Magazine of History,* XLVII (Summer, 1964), 309-18.

MYERS, GUSTAVUS. *The History of Tammany Hall.* New York, 1917.

NASH, RODERICK. "Victor Berger: Making Marx Respectable." *Wisconsin Magazine of History,* XLVII (Summer, 1964), 301-8.

NORDHOFF, CHARLES. *The Communistic Societies of the United States.* New York, 1965.

NOYES, JOHN HUMPHREY. *American Socialisms.* Philadelphia, 1870.

OBERMANN, KARL. *Joseph Weydemeyer: Pioneer of American Socialism.* New York, 1947.

Selected Bibliography [203]

PANCOAST, ELINOR and ANNE E. LINCOLN. *The Incorrigible Idealist: Robert Dale Owen in America.* Bloomington, Indiana, 1940.

PARKS, EDD WINFIELD. "Dreamer's Vision: Frances Wright at Nashoba (1825-30)." *Tennessee Historical Magazine,* II (Series II) (January, 1932), 75-86.

PERKINS, A. J. G. and THERESA WOLFSON. *Frances Wright, Free Enquirer: The Study of a Temperament.* New York, 1939.

PESSEN, EDWARD. *Most Uncommon Jacksonians: The Radical Leaders of the Early Labor Movement.* Albany, 1967.

————. "Thomas Brothers, Anti-Capitalist Employer." *Pennsylvania History,* XXIV (1957), 321-30.

————. "The Working Men's Movement of the Jacksonian Era." *Mississippi Valley Historical Review,* XLIII (December, 1956), 428-43.

PETERSEN, ARNOLD. *Daniel DeLeon: Social Architect.* New York, 1941.

PODMORE, FRANK. *Robert Owen: A Biography.* Two volumes. London, 1906.

POST, ALBERT. *Popular Free Thought In America, 1825-1850.* New York, 1943.

QUINT, HOWARD H. *The Forgoing of American Socialism: Origins of the Modern Movement.* Indianapolis, 1964.

RAYBACK, JOSEPH G. *A History of American Labor.* Rev. ed. New York, 1966.

RIASANOVSKY, NICHOLAS V. *The Teaching of Charles Fourier.* Berkeley, 1969.

RIEGAL, ROBERT E. *American Feminists.* Lawrence, Kansas, 1963.

RISCHIN, MOSES. *The Promised City: New York's Jews, 1870-1914.* New York, 1970.

ROCKER, RUDOLF. *Johann Most: Das Leben eines Rebellen.* Berlin, 1924.

RODMAN, JANE. "The English Settlement in Southern Illinois, 1815-1825." *Indiana Magazine of History,* XLIII (1947), 329-61.

ROGOFF, HARRY. *An East Side Epic: The Life and Work of Meyer London.* New York, 1930.

ROPER, LAURA WOOD. "Frederick Law Olmsted and the Western Texas Free-Soil Movement." *American Historical Review,* LVI (October, 1950), 58-64.

ROSEBLOOM, EUGENE H. *The Civil War Era, 1859-1873,* Vol. IV of *The History of the State of Ohio.* Ed. Carl Wittke. Columbus, 1944.

SAVETH, EDWARD N. *American Historians and European Immigrants, 1875-1925.* New York, 1965.

SCHLÜTER, HERMAN. *Die Anfänge der deutschen Arbeiterbewegung in Amerika.* Stuttgart, 1907.

————. *Die Internationale in Amerika.* Chicago, 1918.

SCHULZ-BEHREND, GEORGE. "Communia, Iowa, a Nineteenth Century German-American Utopia." *Iowa Journal of History,* XLVIII (1950), 27-54.

SHANNON, DAVID A. *The Socialist Party of America.* Chicago, 1967.

SHAW, ALBERT. *Icaria: A Chapter in the History of Communism.* New York, 1884.

SINCLAIR, ANDREW. *The Better Half: The Emancipation of the American Woman.* New York, 1965.

STIERLIN, L. *Der Staat Kentucky und die Stadt Louisville mit besonderer Berücksichtigung des Deutschen Elements.* Louisville, 1873.

STOLBERG, BENJAMIN. *Tailor's Progress: The Story of a Famous Union and the Men Who Made It.* New York, 1944.

SUGGS, GEORGE C., JR. "Catalyst for Industrial Change: The WFM, 1893-1903." *Colorado Magazine,* XLV, 1968.

SUHL, YURI. *Ernestine Rose and the Battle for Human Rights.* New York, 1959.

THERNSTROM, STEPHEN. *Poverty and Progress: Social Mobility in a Nineteenth Century City.* New York, 1969.

THISTLETHWAITE, FRANK. "Migration from Europe Overseas in the Nineteenth and Twentieth Centuries." *New Perspectives on the American Past.* Eds. Stanley N. Katz and Stanley I. Kutler. Boston, 1969.

THOMPSON, E. P. *The Making of the English Working Class.* London, 1963.

VECOLI, RUDOLPH J. "Contadini in Chicago: A Critique of *The Uprooted.*" *Journal of American History,* LI (December, 1964), 404-17.

WACHMAN, MARVIN. *History of the Social-Democratic Party of Milwaukee, 1897-1910.* Urbana, 1945.

WARE, NORMAN. *The Industrial Worker, 1840-1860: The Reaction of American Industrial Society to the Advance of the Industrial Revolution.* Chicago, 1964.

WATERMAN, WILLIAM RANDALL. "Frances Wright." *Columbia University Studies in History, Economics, and Public Law* (CXV), 1924.

WEINSTEIN, JAMES. *The Decline of Socialism in America, 1912-1925.* New York, 1967.

WEISBERGER, BERNARD A. *The New Industrial State.* New York, 1969.

WILSON, WILLIAM E. *The Angel and the Serpent.* Bloomington, 1964.

WITTKE, CARL. *Against the Current: The Life of Karl Heinzen.* Chicago, 1945.

——————. "Friedrich Hassaurek: Cincinnati's Leading Forty-Eighter." *The Ohio Historical Quarterly,* LXVIII (1959).

——————. *The German Language Press in America.* Lexington, 1957.

——————. *Refugees of Revolution: The German Forty-Eighters in America.* Philadelphia, 1952.

——————. *The Utopian Communist: A Biography of Wilhelm Weitling.* Baton Rouge, Louisiana, 1950.

——————. *We Who Built America.* Rev. ed. Cleveland, 1967.

WOOLEN, EVAN. "Labor Troubles Between 1834 and 1837." *Yale Review,* I (May, 1892), 87-100.

YEARLEY, CLIFTON K., JR. *Britons in American Labor: A History of the Influence of the United Kingdom Immigrants in American Labor, 1890-1914.* Baltimore, 1957.

ZAHLER, HELEN SARA. *Eastern Workingmen and National Land Policy, 1829-1862.* New York, 1941.

ZARETZ, CHARLES ELBERT. *The Amalgamated Clothing Workers of America: A Study in Progressive Trade Unionism.* New York, 1934.

ZUCKER, A. E. "Carl Heinrich Schnauffer." *Proceedings of the Annual Meeting of the Society of the History of Germans in Maryland.* 1939.

——————, ed. *The Forty-Eighters: Political Refugees of the German Revolutions of 1848.* New York, 1950.

DISSERTATIONS

BREWER, KARA P. "The American Career of James Connolly." Unpublished M.A. thesis, University of the Pacific, 1972.

IVERSON, ROBERT WILLIAM. "Morris Hillquit: American Social Democrat." Unpublished Ph.D. Dissertation. State University of Iowa, 1951.

MUZIK, EDWARD J. "Victor L. Berger, A Biography." Unpublished Ph.D. Dissertation. Northwestern University, 1960.

Index